LESSONS FROM NEW AMERICAN SCHOOLS' SCALE-UP PHASE

Prospects for Bringing Designs to Multiple Schools

Susan J. Bodilly

with

Brent Keltner ◆ Susanna Purnell
Robert Reichardt ◆ Gina Schuyler

Supported by
New American Schools

RAND Education

RAND

The New American Schools (known as the New American Schools Development Corporation from 1991 through 1995) is a private non-profit corporation, created in conjunction with the America 2000 initiative, to fund the development of new, whole-school designs for elementary and secondary schools that could eventually be adopted in schools across the country. After three years of development and demonstration, NAS chose seven design teams to begin a five-year effort to promote their designs in multiple schools within a district and within multiple districts.

During this time, RAND provided analytic support to NAS. RAND performed an analysis of implementation in the demonstration schools from 1993 to 1995, which is reported in *Lessons from New American Schools Development Corporation's Demonstration Phase* (Bodilly et al., 1996). In the scale-up phase, RAND is conducting both qualitative and quantitative analyses to better understand the effects of the reform on schools and students.

This report documents the findings from the implementation analysis of the first two years (1995–1997) of the five-year scale-up phase. This report should interest educational policymakers at all levels of government, school administrators and teachers, and communities concerned with improved schooling. The research was supported by NAS with funds donated by several foundations: The Ford Foundation, the John S. and James L. Knight Foundation, the John D. and Catherine T. Mac Arthur Foundation, The Pew Charitable Trusts, and others. The study was conducted under the auspices of RAND Education.

CONTENTS

FIGURES

TABLES

In July 1991, NAS, a nonprofit corporation funded by the private sector was established to help existing schools transform themselves into high-performing organizations. The means for achieving this transformation has been the use of whole-school designs and design teams that partner with schools to lend assistance in change. NAS has had four stages: a competition phase, a phase for further design development, a demonstration phase, and a scale-up phase.

This report is a formative assessment of the first two years (1995-1997) of the scale-up phase. The term *scale-up* describes the NAS partnership with ten jurisdictions to increase significantly the number of schools within those jurisdictions that are design-based—that adopt NAS designs to help improve student performance. The NAS concept of scale-up includes both increasing the number of schools using the designs and having a critical mass of design-based schools within the ten jurisdictions.

RESEARCH QUESTIONS

NAS asked RAND to perform several research tasks during the scale-up phase. This document addresses only one of those tasks. The questions addressed in this formative assessment are:

1. Did schools implement the designs and to what extent?

2. Why did some schools make more progress than others toward implementation goals?

METHODOLOGY

RAND used case studies of schools embedded in districts to determine the answers to the above questions. It visited a sample of 40 schools in seven districts, reviewed documents, interviewed school and district staff, and observed some school activities. This data collection and analysis process was intended to determine the level of implementation in each school and what had encouraged it or impeded it. On the basis of these data, we estimated the level of design implementation in each school. Each school's implementation level was assessed against the particular design being adopted. Selection factors, design and team factors, school structural factors, and district and institutional factors were analyzed to understand their effects on the school's level of implementation.

FINDINGS

Our analysis showed significant variation among the schools in the level of implementation obtained, which ranged from no implementation through the stages of planning, piloting, implementing, and fulfilling. Approximately 50 percent of the schools in the sample were at the implementing and fulfilling levels; the others were at lower levels of implementation. Of the 33 schools in the sample that had been implementing for two years, 18 (approximately 54 percent) were at the two highest levels. However, 15 schools in the second year of implementation (close to 45 percent) were still below this level. Of the seven schools in the sample with only one year of implementation, three (43 percent) were at least at the piloting phase.

Selection Process and School Climate Factors

We found that the initial selection process in most districts was hurried and did not always proceed as planned. But some schools fared better than others in this process. In particular, schools were likely to make more significant implementation progress within the two-year time frame we studied if they were well informed, had a free choice among designs, and did not have strife or a leadership turnover. The findings point to the importance of this initiation process and also to its fragility and easy displacement by other district and school priorities. NAS and the partner districts have already significantly changed the selection process in an attempt to promote free, informed choice of designs by schools.

Design and Team Factors

Our observations reveal that the design teams varied in their ability to provide strong implementation support to the increased number of schools in this phase. Higher levels of implementation were associated with design teams that had stable leadership and had created the staff capacity (numbers and quality of staff) to serve the schools; effectively communicated the designs to schools; gained resources from districts for implementation; emphasized curriculum, instruction, student assignment, assessments, and professional development; and supported implementation with whole-school training, facilitators, extensive training days, and common planning time. NAS is currently working with its teams to increase their capabilities for the future.

School Structure and Site Factors

We found implementation was slower in the secondary grades than in the elementary grades. Stronger progress was made in alternative or restructured secondary schools than in "typically" structured secondary schools.

District and Institutional Factors

Analysis of districts and their effects on level of implementation showed that teachers and principals thought both political and structural factors affected implementation. Higher levels of implementation were associated with districts that had stable leadership supportive of the effort, that lacked political crises, that had a culture of trust between the central office and the schools, that provided some school-level autonomy, and that provided resources for professional development and planning.

In many instances the move toward a more supportive environment was delayed by actions other than those of the districts, such as rules and regulations of the states. The effort was delayed in several instances by overwhelming political issues, leadership turnover, elections, and crisis. Finally, at least some part of the pace of restructuring was due to the scale of the effort. Because all schools would be potentially affected, districts reviewed policies and practices extensively and deliberately.

Again, NAS and the partner districts have plans under way intended to improve the support provided to schools.

THEMES AND LESSONS

Several themes come from this analysis. These themes buttress and are buttressed by similar themes from other studies of implementing systemic change in general and in K–12 education in particular:

1. The effort at school reform is complex because of the multiple actors involved, no single one of which controls all the inputs needed to ensure implementation outcomes. The multiplicity of actors in the system targeted for change and their different levels of authority lead to slow progress.

2. Design teams by themselves do not accomplish implementation. Results depend at least in part on inputs that schools and districts control or contribute: resources, commitment, time, and effort.

3. The accomplishments are slow to materialize and are often fleeting because of the political nature of the system in which K–12 education is embedded. Local community issues and district politics—changes in leadership, budget crisis—have an effect and lead inevitably to adjustments and slowed pace.

4. A stable leadership at both the school and district levels appeared to be important to teachers, as were clear signals about the priority to be placed on the effort. But it was the *observed* leadership by operators at the school level that proved crucial. They found messages in many different mechanisms, not just through the verbal statements of leaders. Resource allocation was a particularly important message carrier.

Perhaps the most important lesson we have learned (and one we all learn over and over again) is that there still are no easy answers, no silver bullets. Elmore and McLaughlin (1988) had it right: K–12 reform is steady work. Much needs to be done to ensure that what we observed at the two-year point of the NAS scale-up evolves to the advantage of students and schools. NAS, its design teams, and partner jurisdictions are making changes designed to improve their progress toward the goal of high-performing schools. The formative nature of this report emphasizes that the work has only just begun.

ACKNOWLEDGMENTS

We would like to thank New American Schools, The Ford Foundation, the John S. and James L. Knight Foundation, the John D. and Catherine T. Mac Arthur Foundation, The Pew Charitable Trusts, and other donors for their support of our work. This report would not have been possible without the aid and cooperation of the design teams, districts, and schools involved in the NAS initiative. People in each organization gave freely of their time to enable us to understand the issues involved in implementing whole-school designs in multiple schools within a district and across multiple districts. We thank them for their efforts and also for their dedication to improving the educational prospects of all children. We would also like to thank the many reviewers of this report, especially Tora Bikson and Mike Timpane.

Many wonderful people have participated in the NAS effort since it began in 1991. Several have not lived to see the full fruit of their labor on behalf of this nation's children. We dedicate this report to their memory and the work they did. In particular, we remember with fondness and gratitude Helen Bernstein, Audrey Cohen, Elspeth Kehl, and Joe Miller.

ABBREVIATIONS

AC	Audrey Cohen College System of Education
AT	Authentic Teaching, Learning and Assessment
CN	Co-NECT
EL	Expeditionary Learning
MR	Modern Red Schoolhouse
NA	National Alliance for Restructuring Education
NAS	New American Schools
NASDC	New American Schools Development Corporation
RW	Roots and Wings

Chapter One

INTRODUCTION

This report summarizes RAND's assessment of the New American Schools (NAS) scale-up initiative in school years 1995–96 and 1996–97. In the context of NAS, *scale-up* refers to increasing the number of schools adopting its "whole-school designs" and ensuring that, in some districts, a critical mass of schools adopt these designs.[1] This report offers the public, especially jurisdictions and schools interested in improving their students' performance through school transformation, lessons learned to date from the NAS initiative. The report describes the context of the NAS scale-up effort, methodology used to assess it, the implementation progress made within the two-year period studied, and factors that contributed to that progress. It explores reasons for variation in progress among schools looking at the influence of selection factors, design factors, school factors and district factors on the level of implementation in the schools.

THE IMPLEMENTATION ISSUE IN K–12 REFORM

For many years, K–12 education reformers have been frustrated over the inability to bring about school reforms that lead to improved student outcomes in *many* schools.[2] Letting schools innovate on their own appeared to have limited success, resulting in the adoption of marginal programs, the disappearance of improvements when a

---

[1] This is close to the definition used in Stringfield and Datnow (1998).

[2] We do not provide a literature review of education-reform implementation. The following would be helpful to a reader unacquainted with the field: Berman and McLaughlin (1975), Cuban (1990), Elmore and McLaughlin (1988), Firestone et al. (1989), Smith and O'Day (1990), and Tyack (1990).

principal or sponsor changed, or improvements in one or two schools, but not many. Imposing state and district mandates appeared to offer similar meager successes, with programs disappearing when state and district attention waned or when funding was reduced.[3] The bottom line is that schools and districts have often faddishly adopted new practices only to find them disappear within a short time or remain only in a few selected schools in each district. Thus, a key frustration of those who would improve schools has been the inability to translate the goal of educating all students into coherent school-level responses within *many* schools across the country or even within many schools across a district. We refer to this goal as "scale-up": how to get improved practices into a large number of schools within a specific period of time.

NAS INITIATIVE

NAS is a nonprofit corporation funded by the private sector to develop designs for schools that will enable the schools to significantly improve student performance. The means NAS chose for achieving this was to create whole-school designs and teams that could lend implementation assistance to schools using those designs.

NAS was founded in July 1991 and committed to a five-year initiative that included a competitive request for proposals (RFP) and design-selection process, further development of designs receiving the awards (July 1992–July 1993), a two-year demonstration period of the designs in real schools (1993–1995), and a scale-up (1995–1997). The results of the first three phases of the NAS initiative have been reported elsewhere.[4] This report concentrates on the scale-up phase.

Prior to the scale-up phase, NAS design teams worked in unrelated schools chosen by them and located throughout the nation. In the scale-up phase, NAS and the design teams worked jointly to transform the majority of schools within ten specific jurisdictions. Thus, to NAS, the term *scale-up* implies both breadth (an increase in num-

---

[3]The top-down versus bottom-up dilemma has been voiced before; for example, see Usdan and Schwarz in *Education Week* (1994), Wilson (1989), and Stringfield et al. (1997).

[4]Bodilly et al. (1995); Bodilly et al. (1996); Stringfield, Ross, and Smith (1996).

bers of schools in which interventions are taking place) and depth (concentration in confined political-geographic regions). NAS's scale-up definition also means, and this will be stressed throughout this report, that the NAS intervention began to incorporate and involve more "levels" of actors in the scale-up phase than it had in the past phases. These included NAS itself, design teams, schools, districts, and states.

PURPOSE OF THIS REPORT

The purpose of this report is to provide a formative assessment of NAS's scale-up initiative. This report does not stand alone. NAS asked RAND to perform three major research tasks during the scale-up phase: a formative assessment of implementation after two years, an in-depth assessment of changes in classroom practices and student work over a three-year period, and a quantitative analysis of student outcomes and teachers' and principals' attitudes over a five-year period.

This report addresses the first task: provide a formative assessment of the experience of the first two years of scale-up. The research questions addressed in this report are as follows:

1. Did schools implement the designs and to what extent?

2. Are there any patterns indicating why some schools made more progress than others toward implementation goals?

COMPLEXITY AND UNCERTAINTY AS A THEME OF THE ANALYSIS

An overarching theme emerged from the analysis driven by the above research questions. The NAS efforts at school-level transformation combined complex change, innovative processes, and ambitious time lines for change. These attributes of complexity, innovativeness, and pace had a profound effect on the effort.

First, the NAS effort, as presently construed, involves many different actors: NAS, districts, design teams, schools, teachers, students, parents, etc. In this report, we examine the actions taken by some of these different actors to understand how their actions supported or did not support the implementation of the designs in schools. Within the two-year period studied, we found that no single actor was alone responsible for success or for failure of implementation at the school level. Rather, these outcomes depended on a complex series of interactions among the actors studied.

Second, the actors involved in the NAS initiative were new to each other. They struggled to meet the goals of the initiative under trying circumstances using new methods. Many of the design changes made had not been attempted before or had not been attempted in concert with all the other innovations proposed. Our research reveals an initiative in its early stages, one with many mistakes made but with learning in response to those experiences. The NAS we assess here is not the NAS currently operating in the field.

Finally, the actors all worked under deadlines for implementation established by NAS and the districts. Both groups demanded an implementation cycle in schools that would produce significant results within a three-year period and implementation in over 30 percent of the schools in a jurisdiction within a five-year period. It has proven to be a double-edged sword. These deadlines forced quick action and contributed to a confused beginning of the NAS scale-up effort. But this cycle has ensured the effort did not languish, but always pushed forward.

These factors—the complexity of interactions, the innovativeness and newness of the efforts, and the pace of the efforts—affected the implementation results in schools. The story of NAS's early scale-up experience is a story of an evolving process of change. Many suggestions for improvement embedded in this report have already been incorporated by NAS and its partner jurisdictions. The remainder of this report will explore some of these interactions to illuminate the nature of school reform using the NAS approach.

ORGANIZATION OF THE REPORT

The report is organized to provide contextual information to the reader, a description of the dependent variable (level of implementation in schools), and then descriptions of the impact of independent variables on the dependent one. Chapter Two provides the reader with more details about the NAS scale-up strategy and especially about the challenges inherent in the strategy. This contextual description is very important to understanding the extent of implementation in schools, as well as to understanding the rationale for the research methods. Chapter Three provides the research methods developed in response to the NAS strategy. Chapter Four provides more detail about the criteria we used for gauging school progress and estimates general levels of progress made by the 40 schools included in the sample. Chapters Five, Six, Seven, and Eight explore the effects of different independent variables on the levels of implementation progress in the sample. These independent variables include the selection process by which the school and design team were matched, the factors associated with the design or design-team support, the factors associated with the school site, and the factors associated with the districts involved. Chapter Nine draws out lessons learned.

Appendix A provides details about previous phases of the NAS initiative. Appendix B provides a synopsis of each of the designs.

CAVEATS

Chapter Three will present the caveats to this analysis in more detail. But from the beginning, the reader should be guided by an important one that covers the entire RAND analysis, not just what is reported here. The research reported here is adapted to the complex realities of an unfolding initiative in real schools and real districts. Each of the pieces of the RAND research is necessary, but not sufficient, for a full understanding of the NAS initiative. The enormous complexity of the phenomena under review drives us to a mix of research methods—significant fieldwork and case studies of schools, classroom observations, statistical analysis of student outcomes, surveys of teachers' and principals' attitudes and opinions, analysis of the sources and uses of funds—only some of which are reported here.

The RAND analyses of NAS do not emphasize an experimental design or carefully selected comparison groups. Thus, definitive statements about cause and effect will elude us after the research is complete. However, any deficiencies in methodological finesse are more than compensated for by the in-depth understanding of all the different components of the initiative that our approach provides, by the ability to draw out the general relationships between the many parts (systems analysis), and by the illumination it brings to real practice in real situations.

This report, in particular, is written to help the general public understand the nature of the initiative and the difficulties involved in gaining success from the point of view of the actors involved in it. The report now turns to a description of the initiative.

Chapter Two

HISTORY OF NAS AND THE SCALE-UP STRATEGY

This chapter reviews NAS's purposes and strategy. It emphasizes the scale-up phase; more details about the previous phases are contained in Appendix A. The chapter concludes with a set of tensions or challenges inherent in the NAS approach that provide context for the implementation at the school level.

THE FOUNDING OF NAS AND ITS ROLE IN REFORM

NAS was a prominent part of President Bush's America 2000 educational initiative announced by Secretary of Education Lamar Alexander in April 1991.[1] The proposal followed an agreement on a set of national goals for education between the President and the National Governors Association, a forum presided over by then-Governor Bill Clinton. Among other things, America 2000 proposed the development of voluntary national standards in major subject areas and called for the creation of America 2000 communities that would marshal resources to support the development of high-performance schools. Originally, a third component of the strategy was to provide federal funds ($535 million) to create demonstration schools using break-the-mold practices in each congressional district. These schools would act as lighthouses for reform efforts—the bottom-up component of the reform. However, the last idea never gathered significant congressional support. Instead, the proposal Alexander outlined relied on private-sector funding for the development of break-the-mold designs.

---

[1]U.S. Department of Education (1991).

In July 1991, in conjunction with President Bush's America 2000 initiative, the New American Schools Development Corporation was established as a nonprofit corporation funded by the private sector to create and support design teams capable of helping existing schools transform themselves into high-performing organizations by using whole-school designs.[2] President Clinton later endorsed NAS's work, in keeping with his administration's Goals 2000.

NAS's main goal has always been to increase student performance. The means for achieving this has changed somewhat over time, but one consistent element is that NAS was founded to establish school designs that could be adopted by communities around the nation.[3] NAS hoped to engage the nation's best educators, business people, and researchers in the deliberate and thoughtful creation of teams to develop and demonstrate whole-school designs to enable improved student performance. Other NAS principles constituting its model of change are found in Table 2.1.

NEW AMERICAN SCHOOLS PHASES

The NAS initiative has had four stages, as shown in Figure 2.1. It ran a competition and selected 11 teams with unique designs. It committed to a five-year plan for development, demonstration, and scale-up through the year 1997. After a year of further development, NAS funded nine of the 11 teams to demonstrate and implement whole-school designs in real schools in school years 1993–94 through 1994–95. During this time, the number of NAS schools grew to 147. In school years 1995–96 and 1996–97, NAS continued working closely with seven of the teams to begin a five-year scale-up effort—working closely with more schools to adopt the designs. By the end of the first two years of scale-up, NAS was working with 557 schools. This five-year commitment overlapped with the last two years of the original commitment, thus moving NAS's timeline out to the year 2000. By fall 1997, NAS grew to 685 associated schools and is predicting growth to over 1,000 schools in the next few years.

---

[2]The name was shortened to New American Schools (NAS) in 1995 to reflect the end of the development phase. In this document, we will refer to the organization as NAS.

[3]New American Schools Development Corporation (1991), p. 35.

Table 2.1

Original NAS Principles and Concepts

Principle	Description
Private Funding	The effort was privately funded and supported—it was not a government mandate. Ideally, schools and districts would enter into a relationship with a design team on a voluntary and well-informed basis.
Whole School	Designs were to be for "whole schools." This notion had two parts. First, the designs would be coherent, thoughtful sets of school-level policies and practices. The adoption and adept use of coherent, interrelated, and mutually reinforcing practices would be the antithesis of the fragmented programs and idiosyncratic teacher practices often found in schools. In addition, designs were to be for all students. They were not special programs targeted on specific populations to be added to the school's repertoire.
Adaptive Approach	NAS designs were not supposed to be prescriptive molds for model schools to ensure uniformity of practice. Designs were to adapt to local conditions and were to enable local communities to create their own high-performance schools.
Design Teams	Teams were deliberately created organizations of experts. NAS intended that teams would develop coherent designs and then work with schools in further ground-level product development to perfect those designs. Later, they would promote the use of their designs in schools across the nation. Over 600 potential teams responded to the RFP. The 11 initially chosen were mostly private nonprofit organizations connected to universities or research organizations. The exceptions were one for-profit firm, two districts, and one nonprofit without a research or university connection.
Multiple Designs	There was no one best school design, but many, depending on the needs of individual schools. Multiple teams would be supported, allowing schools a choice of designs.
Reasonable Costs	While it was understood that transforming schools might require investment funding, the operating costs of the schools after transformation were to be equivalent to those for the "typical" school in that community. In other words, break-the-mold designs were to be no more costly in daily operation than other schools, making them affordable to all districts.
Market-Driven	NAS would not be a self-perpetuating organization. From the beginning, it planned to "go out of business" after it had accomplished its purpose. One consequence of this was that design teams had to become financially self-sufficient over time, creating their own client base to support their work. Thus, teams over the five-year time line to which NAS originally committed (1992–1997) would need to transform themselves from visionaries, to product developers, to entrepreneurial organizations.

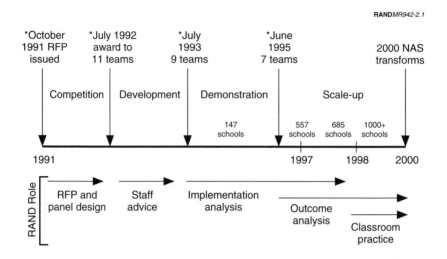

Figure 2.1—NAS Evolution and RAND Role

NAS had not deeply considered what scale-up meant during its early years. But as the fall of 1995 approached, NAS began to consider its product and its potential market seriously. From these discussions, several major shifts emerged that together constitute the "scale-up strategy." These include a shift in design teams, a shift in the product, a new focus, and a new basis for revenue generation. Each is discussed below.

SCALE-UP PRODUCT

NAS's product had changed when it moved into the scale-up phase in terms of the teams entering the phase, the product they offered, and their base of revenues.

Design Teams

An important finding from the demonstration phase was that the teams varied greatly in their ability to demonstrate their designs. Several teams were still missing important components; others were in the midst of restructuring or revising the designs and implementation assistance. At that point, NAS dropped two teams, primarily because it judged that they were not ready to go to scale-up. The remaining seven teams had not demonstrated their concepts in equal depth, but NAS judged that they were at least prepared for the next step. The seven teams are described in Appendix B and explained in detail in previous work.[4] The teams are

- Audrey Cohen College System of Education (AC)

- ATLAS (Authentic Teaching, Learning, and Assessment of All Students) Communities (AT)

- Co-NECT Schools (CN)

- Expeditionary Learning Outward Bound (EL)

- Modern Red Schoolhouse (MR)

- National Alliance for Restructuring Education (NA)

- Roots and Wings (RW).

Design-Based Assistance

The single strongest lesson learned from the demonstration experience was that designs, by themselves, could not transform schools. Schools could not simply open an envelope with design specifications inside and transform themselves. Rather, schools needed significant amounts of professional development and materials geared to the design. Thus, the designs and their implementation assistance packages were the important products developed in the demonstration phase.

This came to be called design-based assistance, and the design teams changed to assistance organizations. NAS began to market design-based assistance to potential clients as the product of the scale-up phase. The term is meant to include materials and products that describe the school design and teaching tasks; a plan for enabling a school to learn about and adopt a design, including training and professional development plans; and design team staff to assist and guide the school through its transformation.

---

[4]Bodilly et al. (1996) and Bodilly et al. (1995).

Fee-for-Service

As intended, the NAS financial support for design teams shrunk throughout the two years of scale-up studied. Starting in the scale-up phase, the design teams went to a "fee-for-service" approach. They all began to charge for their services to schools. Resources for implementation and fees were to come from the schools or their associated districts.

MARKET DEFINITION

NAS developed a two-pronged approach to marketing its designs: opportunistic adoption of designs by schools and a focused expansion in specific jurisdictions.[5]

Opportunistic Non-Jurisdiction Approach

One part of the scale-up strategy simply encouraged the design teams to go to schools that were interested in them. This school-by-school expansion was controlled by teams and was not controlled or overseen by NAS in any way. By the end of the second year of the scale-up phase, about one-quarter of the 550 or so schools involved with NAS were in schools scattered across the country. These schools are primarily associated with the RW and the NA designs.

Jurisdiction Approach

The main focus of expansion, and the new model for change (see Figure 2.2), was a break from the past. NAS was convinced that its designs would not become permanent in districts unless the districts offered a more supportive environment. Just as importantly, it began to ask the question, "why is it we can find a few good schools in every district, but no district where good schools are the norm?"[6] Leaders at NAS—influenced by such reformers as David Hornbeck, Mike Strembinski, and Paul Hill and restructuring experiences in Ken-

---

[5]*Jurisdictions* generally means districts. But NAS has partnered with several states and specific districts in those states. We call these *jurisdiction partners* as well.

[6]This question has been asked by others (Meier, 1998).

RAND*MR942-2.2*

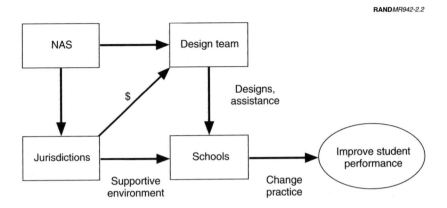

Figure 2.2—Interrelationship in NAS Scale-Up

tucky, Miami, and Chicago—began to embrace the philosophy that district-level restructuring was necessary to a coherent strategy for school reform—one that incorporated both "top-down" and "bottom-up" changes.

In addition, one of NAS's design teams, NA, had developed such a strategy. Its approach was twofold: (1) develop and work with a district-level field team to provide leadership for the school-level work; and (2) provide direct support to schools in their efforts to implement change around the five design tasks. Using this model, NA joined in partnerships with several districts to transform district and school practices, including districts in California, Washington, Kentucky, and Pennsylvania. The NA philosophy of reform also influenced thinking at NAS.

Given these influences, NAS announced that the major emphasis of its scale-up strategy would be to work closely with a few jurisdictions to transform at least 30 percent of the schools in each of those jurisdictions within a five-year period using design-based assistance. Note that this automatically stretched the NAS initiative out three years, to the year 2000.

NAS hoped to partner with districts that had undergone significant prior restructuring. In partnership with NAS, the district would continue to become supportive of whole-school transformation.

Supportive had clear meaning in NAS's view, as articulated in a "strategy paper" in 1995 that was sent to all jurisdictions interested in a partnership with NAS.[7] The ten attributes of a supportive environment that NAS proposed are listed in Table 2.2. While the strategy paper enumerated these ten aspects of a supportive environment, NAS in practice quickly focused on a smaller number that included investment funding for change; school autonomy from district rules and regulations; a coherent and funded plan for professional development; a push toward public engagement and support for school change; and appropriate accountability systems that would incentivize teachers, principals, and district representatives toward improved performance.

PARTNER JURISDICTIONS

The jurisdictions were chosen in a closed RFP process. NAS sent letters to 20 or so jurisdictions that had shown interest in the past or were known to one or more of the design teams. The letter asked the district or state to submit a proposal for a partnership. NAS offered a small grant of $250,000 per year for two years to each jurisdiction. In the proposal submitted by the targeted jurisdictions, each claimed a history of significant restructuring and pledged to create an even more supportive environment for school transformation if they partnered with NAS.

NAS chose ten jurisdictions to work with based on the proposals submitted: Cincinnati, Dade County, Kentucky, Maryland, Memphis, Philadelphia, Pittsburgh, San Antonio, San Diego, and a collection of five districts in Washington state. The districts in Kentucky, Pittsburgh, and San Diego were partners with the NA design team, and that team had worked with the district leadership during the previous two years to encourage a supportive environment for school-level transformation.

The districts that chose to partner with NAS do not reflect the national norm or average:

- NAS chose primarily urban districts with dense populations. Districts in Kentucky are the exception; they are rural. Two of

---

[7]New American Schools Development Corporation (1995).

these districts, Dade County and Philadelphia, are among the 20 largest districts in the country. Memphis ranks 21st, San Antonio ranks 56th, Cincinnati ranks 67th, and Pittsburgh ranks 108th.

Table 2.2

NAS Attributes of a Supportive Environment

Attribute	Description
School autonomy	Substantial autonomy should reside with schools over budget allocation within the school, staffing, curriculum, instruction, schedule, student assignment, adding performance standards beyond those required by the district, and demonstrating accountability.
High standards	The district should develop a set of standards for achievement for all students that cover content, skills, and performance.
Appropriate assessments	The district should have a rich set of assessments aligned with the standards, well beyond multiple-choice tests, to help schools assess and understand student competencies.
Sources of assistance	Districts should provide assistance to schools to transform, preferably through design teams, but also through colleges and others.
Professional development	Districts should have a system for design-based professional development and certification responsive to the needs of schools and tied to comprehensive improvement efforts.
Technology	Technology available in the schools should support teachers and students in the instructional process and in the management of school records.
Community services and supports	The community should provide a support system for families that reduces the health and other nonacademic barriers to learning.
Public engagement	Districts should engage the public in the development of standards, programs, services, etc.
Capacity and willingness to invest	The district should build and allocate an investment fund to provide resources to schools for the transition costs of adopting whole-school reforms.
Systems management and governance	The district should adopt, as appropriate, the restructuring of school boards; changes to state-level governance; removal of constraints in collective bargaining contracts and state law, rules, and regulations; reworking of the incentive systems for performance by teachers; and coordination of practices.

- The national average for percentage of children receiving free and reduced-price lunches is about 36 percent. All of these districts exceeded that amount; in five, well in excess of 50 percent received free and reduced-price lunches.

- With the exception of the two districts in Kentucky, the districts all have enrollments with a disproportionate number of minority students compared to national averages (i.e., greater than 50 percent minority).

Thus, the scale-up strategy included a group of partners—jurisdictions—that were expected to create supportive environments and that adopted NAS as a major change strategy for the jurisdiction. This strategy, depicted in Figure 2.2, will have strong direct effects on the outcomes of the effort and increases the number of possible relationships among actors that will affect the outcomes. In the development phase, the main relationship was between NAS and teams. In the demonstration phase, schools became an important part of the action. In the scale-up phase, districts were added to the strategy for change, increasing the possible interrelationships that add to the complexity of the effort and add important political actors that can influence implementation.

MATCHING SCHOOLS TO DESIGNS—THE SELECTION PROCESS

NAS believed that schools needed a choice of designs, and it promoted the notion that schools be allowed an informed choice from among several designs. It proposed an idealized matching process: All schools in the district would receive materials and brochures from each design team. Then, the district would hold a "design-team fair," at which the teams would make presentations to teams of staff from all the schools. In this way, the schools would be introduced to the people they might be working with over the next few years, could ask questions and get responses, and would begin to build a relationship. This initial screening would narrow the slate of teams for each school, so that schools could then ask for follow-up visits from just one or two teams. This could be followed by visits by a school team to a demonstration site of the design team. Finally, NAS and several teams proposed that the school staff vote to accept a design—with a clear majority needed before a partnership could be established.

Teacher unions in several of the partnership districts also required a vote.

In jurisdictions that were already partnering with NA, a similar process would be attempted in later years. Other design teams were welcome to enter into partnerships with schools in those jurisdictions. We note here that, in the jurisdictions of Kentucky and Pittsburgh during the two-year period we studied, schools and districts remained closely partnered with NA.

The concept of choice of design was also promoted as NAS became more collaborative with other whole-school design initiatives, such as Paideia and Accelerated Schools. These and several other "teams" participated in the fairs, at least in part because of the insistence of the districts involved.

THE TIMETABLE FOR MATCHING AND SELECTION

NAS, concerned over letting the momentum of its effort wane, urged a hurried timetable for forming partnerships with the districts and for schools being matched with designs. While the demonstration phase ended in July 1995, NAS wanted the scale-up phase to begin at that point with new jurisdictions in place and new schools beginning to implement the designs. NAS sent out invitations to prospective districts in November 1994. Districts submitted proposals, then NAS visited the most promising respondents during January and February 1995. NAS selected the jurisdictions by March 1995. Because the partnership established the goal of 30 percent of the schools affiliating with NAS designs over the scale-up period, jurisdictions were asked to start at least 10 percent of their schools implementing a design by fall 1995 with significant training of staff during the summer of 1995.

IMPLICATIONS

Inherent in NAS's approach are challenges that have had and will continue to have effects on the implementation outcomes and final student performance outcomes associated with the initiative. These were recognized at the beginning of scale-up and discussed in NAS staff meetings we observed. Thus, they are covered here as a means of summarizing the context of the effort.

First, embedded in the NAS approach is a possible conflict. On the one hand, in the RFP, NAS called for "break-the-mold" designs that ignored existing rules, regulations, and traditions governing schools. On the other hand, in demonstration and scale-up, NAS asked for rapid matching and implementation in existing schools that face very real rules, regulations, and traditions. The story of implementation of NAS designs will be the story of attempting to meet two possibly conflicting goals: being highly innovative and maintaining high quality versus being able to implement rapidly in many existing schools.[8] The main issue confronting "going to scale" is embedded in this possible conflict.

Second, the scale-up strategy NAS adopted can be considered complex. In terms of the implementation literature, this often means that many actors are involved and that these actors can have a strong influence on the progress of the initiative. Importantly, each often controls only part of the decisionmaking process, leading to a "fragmented" policy environment (Lindblom, 1959). The more actors that are involved—especially in the form of organizations and suborganizations with goals, objectives, and procedures that may compete or are not complementary—the more likely it is that implementation will be slow and bumpy.[9] NAS used a concurrent development strategy. Activities of finishing-up demonstrations overlapped with activities concerned with entering into complex agreements with new partners for scale-up. This overlap of efforts added to the level of complexity, requiring NAS and the design teams to deal with two different sets of clients at the same time. In school literature, "complexities of joint action" often result in a phenomenon labeled "mutual adaptation" or "mutual adjustment," in which the implementation slows, and the intervention changes over time.[10]

---

[8]Organizational researchers Wilson (1989) and Daft (1995) have discussed the conflict between being an innovative organization and ensuring a reform can be implemented throughout the organization.

[9]Pressman and Wildavsky (1973) call this "the complexity of joint action"; see also Mazmanian and Sabatier (1989).

[10]Pressman and Wildavsky (1973), Berman and McLaughlin (1975), and Lindblom (1959).

Third, two years were allotted for implementation of NAS demonstration sites—two years to restructure a school significantly; change its organization, staffing, curriculum, and instruction; and demonstrate changes in outcomes. RAND reports on this showed that much implementation remained to be done as teams entered the scale-up phase.[11] In scale-up, RAND reporting is again taking place after just two years. The literature on education reform does not support the view that these kinds of objectives could be obtained in the time provided, no matter the money or effort put into school transformation. While some evidence exists that specific programs can be put in place within this time frame, no studies show that whole-school transformation can be accomplished within two years.

To the contrary, the experience of other reform efforts geared to whole-school transformation indicates that it takes minimally five years, if it can be accomplished at all.[12] As Adelman and Pringle (1995) indicate, "the process of school reform has taken more time than was initially allocated to it." NAS decisionmakers were aware of these concerns from the beginning but felt that the ambitious deadlines would encourage due diligence on the part of teams and schools.

Fourth, the NAS strategy for scale-up is significantly different from most reform efforts of schools. Under the NAS scale-up strategy, schools must provide their own funding, be active participants in the process of change, and be accountable to their districts for the progress made. Within a five-year period, teams had to change from small research organizations dependent on grants into entrepreneurial organizations that are self-sufficient and reach many schools with effective offerings for design-based assistance. This significantly different approach should be expected to create some confusion and initial misunderstanding—the more so, if the com-

---

[11]Bodilly et al. (1996).

[12]Other school-level transformation activities allow schools a longer period to demonstrate changes. Levin (1993) states, "It takes about six years to fully transform a conventional school to accelerated status." Prestine and Bowen (1993, p. 302), in writing on the Coalition of Essential Schools, state that "a minimum of five years was recommended for the entire process." See also Herman and Stringfield (1995) and Policy Studies Associates (1994).

munication of the initiative was not clear to the operators (teachers) responsible for implementing it.[13]

The challenges of the strategy were known fairly early on; their full effects remain uncertain. The ability to implement the strategy, especially under the very real constraints on resources and time, could be seen *a priori* to be problematic. In the remainder of this report, these challenges will be visited again, probing for the extent to which they inhibited the implementation.

---

[13]Pressman and Wildavsky (1973), Mazmanian and Sabatier (1989), and Bodilly et al. (1996).

Chapter Three

RESEARCH APPROACH AND METHODS

This chapter reviews the research approach and methods. It enumerates the research questions, describes the conceptual framework, describes the case study approach used and then lays out the analysis plan.

RAND'S RESEARCH AGENDA

NAS specifically requested that RAND perform five interrelated tasks during the scale-up phase:

- Provide an assessment of the design teams' ability to implement their designs in schools and make progress toward the NAS goals.

- Perform in-depth observations of a sample of NAS classrooms to understand the type of and level of changes that occur. This work, only just being developed, will use comparison schools within a single district to understand the differences in practice and student work that emerge over a three-year period (1998–2000).

- Provide a quantitative analysis of the outcomes associated with schools in the scale-up phase (1995–2000) using a set of outcome indicators including test scores, attendance rates, promotion and continuation rates, etc. This work relies on surveys of teachers and principals in approximately 180 schools as well as collection and analysis of school-level data routinely reported by the districts.

- Track changes made to designs and design-based assistance as a result of "real" implementation experiences.

- Integrate findings into a series of public reports over the life of NAS.

Each of the first four research tasks is necessary to understand the effectiveness of the NAS effort. However, taken together, they are not sufficient to understand the full effects. While these tasks will enable us to answer many questions, definitive answers about the specific nature of cause and effect are likely to escape us.

This document addresses the first task: provide an assessment of the experience of the first two years of scale-up and draw lessons learned. Because it is an early assessment of scale-up, it can provide useful information to all involved about how to improve the process throughout the remainder of scale-up.

RESEARCH QUESTIONS

The extensive school-reform literature indicates that a major problem in school reform is not that the interventions do not have the desired effects, but that the interventions are never implemented so as to have the desired effects.[1] The NAS demonstration phase was designed to work out some of the problems of implementation, ensuring that the design teams had ample opportunity to develop sound implementation strategies for schools. However, scale-up implementation experiences should differ significantly from the demonstration phase for several reasons, including the following: (1) the strategy changed to include important new partners; (2) the teams moved to a different resource base; (3) and the teams scaled up to more sites. Thus, it is appropriate to follow the implementation through the scale-up phase.

The questions addressed in this report are

1. Did schools implement the designs and to what extent?

2. Are there any patterns indicating why some schools made more progress than others toward implementation goals?

---

[1]Berman and McLaughlin (1975); Cuban,(1990); Elmore and McLaughlin (1988); Firestone, Furham, and Kirst (1989); and Shields and Knapp (1997).

CONCEPTUAL FRAMEWORK

The NAS model of change is to use external "change agents" in the form of design teams to intervene in schools and districts to enable schools to change practice, thus eventually changing the student outcomes. Figure 2.2 showed the different actors involved in the process of implementation. Figure 3.1 rearranges these actors into a conceptual framework for the research. The next few paragraphs describe the conceptual framework of this study in more detail.

Dependent Variable

For the purposes of this report, the outcome we are interested in—or the dependent variable—is the level of implementation in the schools implementing NAS designs. This is shown as the central oval in Figure 3.1.

We will discuss the measurement of this variable below, but for now, we focus on one important attribute of this variable: In the education community, there is no agreement on a single best practice. Rather, multiple "best practices" exist that can be pieced together to produce strong effects or weak effects. The hope of NAS is that the design teams have each pieced together best practices or "research-based" practices into a coherent whole. Each design intends to produce strong improvements in different ways. The changed practice

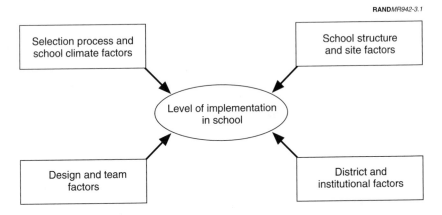

RAND*MR942-3.1*

Figure 3.1—Conceptual Framework of Analysis

in an "ideal type" EL school is different from that of an MR school. This is, after all, the point of having multiple designs.

Thus, the design of the NAS interventions drives us to a simple concept for the dependent variable: *Each design's implementation can only be measured against the attributes of practice that the particular design is trying to imprint upon the school.* Thus, what we observe as implementation must vary by design. School progress toward design implementation must be assessed against that design team's particular goals, objectives, and vision. This means comparing progress across designs must be done cautiously—each is being held to its own standard.

Independent Variables

The NAS intervention in the scale-up phase includes different levels of actors and processes that are likely to influence the dependent variable strongly. Thus, there are several groups of independent variables: a set of variables concerning how schools and teams were matched; a set of variables associated with the design teams or designs; a set of variables associated with the school itself; and a set of variables associated with the district or state, indicated as "institutional context." These are indicated by the boxes surrounding the dependent variable in Figure 3.1. The institutional category includes many factors that are normally included in "the environment," such as changes in state policy, budget crisis, or turnover in leadership.

The NAS strategy by itself indicates that these independent variables would be likely to affect implementation. RAND research in the demonstration phase also indicated that these factors would prove to be important. In fact, the literature on implementation, and school implementation in particular, also indicates that these will be important contributors to implementation and that their effects will be complex and only understood in the unique context of each district and school.

Within these sets of independent variables, many were identified from previous RAND research on NAS during the demonstration phase and have strong backing in the implementation literature. For example, middle schools and high schools face different barriers to schoolwide change than do elementary schools; because of these differences, elementary schools are likely to show higher levels of implementation in shorter periods of time than are the higher grade levels.[2] In addition, the nature of the choice offered to schools in acceptance of a reform and the clarity of the tasks they must undertake will be important.[3] Finally, stable leadership and clear support (through allocation of resources and autonomy) from all levels are listed in primers on implementation research as important contributors to positive implementation, and RAND research on the demonstration phase supported these previous findings.[4] Less trailblazing has taken place on factors relating to the design or design team. Here, we rely more on our own work from the earlier NAS phases.[5]

CASE-STUDY APPROACH

The intervention assessed here is highly complex and embedded in "real" schools in "real" districts. The relationships are so involved and dynamic that they argue against an experimental-design or comparison-group approach. The interventions and research questions argue instead for a replicated case-study approach, with the unit of analysis being the implementing school.

The natural variations we expect to see are connected to the independent variables: the selection process particular to each school, different designs and design teams, different school site factors, and different district and state environments. To provide as much natural contrast and comparison as possible, the replicated cases are embedded within districts, and multiple designs are observed within each district.

SAMPLE

Resources allowed the development of 40 school-level case studies with the intent of performing longitudinal analysis across each

---

[2]Bidwell (1996), Bodilly et al. (1995), McDonald (1995), Newman (1996), Powell (1985), Sebring (1995), and Sizer (1992).

[3]Pressman and Wildavsky (1973), Mazmanian and Sabatier (1989), Bodilly et al. (1996), and Huberman and Miles (1984).

[4]Pressman and Wildavsky (1973), Mazmanian and Sabatier (1989), and Bodilly et al. (1996).

[5]Bodilly et al. (1996).

school over a two-year period. The following paragraphs explain how we chose the sample schools.

NAS is working with 10 jurisdictions, including three state jurisdictions, with specific districts in those states, and seven independent districts.[6] We chose six of these jurisdictions to study in the first year of implementation.[7] We used seven in the second year.[8] That choice was in part determined by the evident progress made in getting the initiative under way in each jurisdiction. At the time the study began, several districts had not negotiated a partnership agreement with NAS.

In choosing schools to study, we attempted to get at least four schools for each design team, to be able to track differences both among designs and among districts. However, each team does not work in each jurisdiction, and each team is implementing in different numbers of schools. For example, AC has less than 20, the fewest schools, while RW has more than 100 schools implementing at least the *Success for All* portion of the design. Neither are the teams uniformly dispersed throughout all districts. For example, Cincinnati has only CN, EL, and RW schools.

Table 3.1 shows the sample for the second year of scale-up. This report is based on the second year sample. Of the 40 schools we visited in 1997, we had also visited 30 in the previous year. Ten were visited only once. Seven of these 10 were visited only once because they were added when we added districts in the second year. Those schools are in San Antonio and Philadelphia.

---

[6]This includes selected districts within the states of Kentucky, Maryland, and Washington and seven districts: Cincinnati, Dade, Memphis, Pittsburgh, Philadelphia, San Antonio, and San Diego.

[7]In the first year, we chose the six jurisdictions to study that had schools that were beginning implementation that year. These included: Cincinnati, Dade, two districts in Kentucky, Memphis City, Pittsburgh City, and two districts in Washington.

[8]In the second year, NAS's relationship with some districts changed; thus, the district sample changed. We added two jurisdictions (Philadelphia and San Antonio) and dropped one (Washington), making seven jurisdictions in the second year: Cincinnati, Dade, two districts in Kentucky, Memphis, Pittsburgh, Philadelphia, and San Antonio. Five jurisdictions stayed the same over the entire study and two new ones were added in the second year.

Table 3.1

RAND Sample for Site Visits

	AC	AT	CN	EL	MR	NA	RW	Totals
Cincinnati			2	2			2	6
Dade	1		2		2		2	7
Kentucky						4		4
Memphis	2	2	1	2	2		2	11
Philadelphia		3	1		1			5
Pittsburgh						3		3
San Antonio				2	2			4
Totals	3	5	6	6	7	7	6	40

We attempted to make the choice of schools within a district random. In at least one case, we had little choice but to leave the selection to the district.[9] While not random, our sample is fairly representative of NAS schools in general. The sample includes urban and rural schools and districts; elementary schools, middle schools, and high schools; and schools that were well-resourced and schools that were not.

DATA SOURCES AND COLLECTION

We used many sources and types of information as outlined in Table 3.2:

- Structured interviews (a set of predefined questions, both open and closed ended), by telephone about resource usage and in person during field visits. The structured formats varied by type of respondent.

- Observations of activities in schools. These observations were not formal or extensive. We toured each of the schools, sat in on several randomly selected classes, and observed special events at

---

[9]For example, the state of Florida put a group of Dade County schools on a probation list because of low performance against a set of state indicators. Dade County mandated that all schools on this list adopt the RW design and be off-limits to researchers. Thus, this group could not be included in the sample, leaving us with no choice as to which RW schools to include—the only two RW schools not on the state probation list.

Table 3.2

Data Types and Sources

	Structured Interviews			Archival			
	In Person	Phone	Observations	Document	Plans	News	Numeric Data
NAS	✓		✓	✓	✓		✓
National design teams	✓	✓		✓	✓	✓	✓
Local design team representatives	✓						
District				✓	✓	✓	✓
Superintendent	✓						
Coordinators	✓	✓					
Title 1	✓						
Budget	✓						✓
School			✓a	✓	✓	✓	✓
Principals	✓	✓					
Facilitators	✓						
Teacher group	✓						
Lead teachers	✓						
Classrooms			✓				
Union	✓						
State Representatives	✓b						

aLimited.

bWhen the state was the primary partner with NAS (Kentucky).

the school scheduled for the day, if they had applications to the design. In several instances we were able to observe critical friends' visits taking place, teacher group meetings, etc.

- Archival data, including documents produced by design teams, schools, and districts describing their efforts; plans by these parties for transformation; and local news releases or newspaper items concerning the local education scene, local political issues, NAS, design teams, or schools using NAS designs.

- Numerical data on each school's enrollment, demographics, test scores, etc.

The major data collection in the field took place during two waves of site visits in spring 1996 and in spring 1997. The latter established the level of implementation of the 40 schools at the end of the second year of scale-up. All interviews probed for the reasons behind differing levels of implementation.

We attempted to ensure that two researchers visited each school for approximately one day. One researcher spent a day at the district collecting information and performing interviews. All interviews had a structured format, with a mix of factual closed-ended questions and open-ended questions. Interviews were translated into condensed formatted sheets that covered specific variables identified to be of interest and coded for later analysis. Specific issues, such as resource usage and the matching process between design teams and schools, were explored using structured phone surveys.

ANALYSIS PLAN

The analysis mixes quantitative and qualitative measures. We used the qualitative data to develop a quantitative measure for the dependent variable, the level of implementation. The independent variables remain largely qualitative.

Measuring the Dependent Variable

The implementation analysis used an auditlike approach to establish the level of implementation in each school. Schools associated with each team were assessed over common areas of schooling we call elements (see Table 3.3). By *common*, we mean that each design included specific changes to that element from "typical" practice.

These common elements were curriculum, instruction, assessments, student assignments, and professional development. But within each element of schooling, the teams varied significantly in what they attempted to accomplish.

For example, while AC, EL, and RW address and expect significant changes in student assignment, student assignment has different meanings among these designs. For the AC design, students can be assigned as they normally are into classrooms; however, within the

Table 3.3

Elements of Designs

Element	Description
Curriculum	Usually, the knowledge bases and the sequence in which they are covered, whether defined by traditional subject areas or in more interdisciplinary fashion.
Instruction	The manner in which the student acquires knowledge and the role of the teacher in this process.
Assessments	The means for measuring progress toward standards, either at the school or student level.
Student Grouping	The criteria or basis for assigning students to classes, groups, programs.
Professional Development	Includes opportunities to develop curriculum and instruction, to develop expertise in using standards, to collaborate with others, and to enter into networks or prolonged discussions with other teachers about the profession. Several teams also planned extensive on-the-job practice, coaching in the classroom, and teaming in individual classrooms, as well as schoolwide forums to change the ways in which teachers deliver curriculum and instruction permanently.
Community Involvement/ Public Engagement	The ways parents, businesses, and others participate in schools and vice versa.
Standards	The range of skills and content areas a student is expected to master to progress through the system and the levels of attainment necessary for schools to be judged effective.
Staff and Organization	The configuration of roles and responsibilities of different staff. Changed organizational structures and incentives encourage teachers to access both staff inservices and professional growth opportunities.

classroom, one would expect to see significant group work on projects and constructive actions, cooperative learning, and flexible grouping according to the task. In EL schools, students are detracked at the classroom level, and teachers have the same students at least two years in a row. The RW design includes a 90-minute period for reading and language arts, with homogeneous grouping by ability level that remains flexible according to student performance, which is assessed every eight weeks. RW uses heterogeneous groupings, potentially across grade levels, for the 90-minute integrated social science and science curriculum known as World Lab.

Three elements remained, but were not held in common among the teams: staff and organization, community involvement, and standards. That is, not all teams aspired to make significant changes in these areas. Together with the five common ones, these are the eight elements that make up what we refer to as the school-level component of the designs. We also tracked progress on these three elements, as applicable.[10]

The specifics of each element for each design team were originally determined by a document review and interview with the design team during the demonstration phase. The elements were sharpened in scale-up by a request from NAS and several districts for design teams to create "benchmarks" of progress for their designs that schools and districts could use to understand where they were going and when and to determine whether they were making reasonable progress. The benchmarks developed varied significantly from team to team as one would expect; however, all gave descriptions of what teams expected by the final year of a three-year implementation cycle.

We relied on two types of evidence of progress. First, we looked for evidence of implementation in keeping with the benchmarks and

---

[10]Our analysis of design documents shows that, in fact, the teams have more elements than these eight. Additional elements include governance changes, integrated technology in the classroom, and integrated social services. In scale-up, with the emphasis on developing a supportive environment within the district, these elements became part of NAS's jurisdiction strategy: all of the governance, integrated social services, and technology. We thus still tracked them, but not as part of the school-level designs. Instead, we tracked them as part of the jurisdiction's supportive environment that NAS was to encourage and support.

expectations provided by the team. Second, we interviewed district and school-level staff to understand their views of the design and how much they had changed their behaviors and to gain descriptions of the level of implementation. We asked how much their jobs had changed so far in relation to where they understood the design to be taking them.

Measuring the Independent Variables

Through our structured interviews and document review, we attempted to understand what contributed to different levels of progress. Our structured interviews had embedded hypotheses, as indicated above, about the relationships that might exist. For example, we took some time in structured interviews with teachers to understand their views of the selection process and how it affected their subsequent implementation behavior. However, we used open-ended questions to allow respondents to insert their own understandings. Specifically, we asked district and school staff about their relationships with the teams; whether the support they needed for transformation was forthcoming; and any rules, regulations, or district policies that had been helpful or were a hindrance. Finally, we asked what needed to be changed to really push the effort to deeper levels of implementation.

Responses from different organizational levels were checked with the district representatives in a feedback session to determine whether the barriers schools reported were real.

Some of the independent variables are quantitative, and their measurement was straightforward. For example, we used the percentage of students receiving free and reduced-price lunches, as reported by the district and the school, as a socioeconomic measure for the school. We used the actual resources expended in particular categories, as reported in interviews of principals, districts, and design teams, to understand the resource support for the design in a district.

Other variables are more qualitative; for these, we used simple categories to assign the school to one circumstance or another (a dummy variable). For example, we asked school staff if they were forced to take a design. If the majority said yes, we assigned this school to the "forced match" category. If the majority did not, then the school was assigned to the "not forced" category.

Some district factors and design factors used similar types of qualitative statements, but the value of the variable for each district or design was arrived at by comparing the members of the group in question. For example, some of the design factors rely on a comparison of the emphasis of each team on certain practices. The variable falls in a category of either emphasized or not emphasized, as compared to the other teams. Some district-level factors take on values on a simple scale of low, medium, high in terms of the extent that the factor was present at the site, as determined by a content review of interviews and document reviews.

Analysis

In the analysis, we simply took the quantitative measure of implementation level for schools and arrayed it against specific values of the independent variables. This provided a means of identifying important relationships and patterns of association. We then referred to specific interviews or documents to provide a deeper understanding. After several interactions, we settled on the most concise means for displaying the themes that emerged and highlighting the most important relationships. Chapters Five through Eight provide rich detail from interviews to show the interrelationships among the variables.

CAVEATS

The following specific caveats apply to the analysis:

- This analysis was not based on a random sample. Selection biases exist for both districts and schools. Their exact nature is not known.

- The independent variables are likely to have a high degree of interdependence.

- The implementation is only the first step in the process of transformation. The proof of the NAS approach is not in these data, but will be revealed in the next few years as it is determined whether this progress had a permanent or fleeting effect on student performance.

Chapter Four

FINDINGS ON PROGRESS TOWARD
IMPLEMENTATION

This chapter summarizes our findings on the level of implementation observed at the 40 schools in the RAND implementation sample. The chapter first shows the creation of the scale for level of implementation, the dependent variable. It then displays the general findings.

The findings presented below will display progress using both five and eight elements, whichever is most appropriate for the discussion. In addition, we separate out the seven schools in their first year of implementation (herein known as year 1 schools) from the 33 schools in their second year of implementation (herein known as year 2 schools) to show the different levels of progress involved.

CREATING A SCALE

The following paragraphs describe the construction of the dependent variable of the analysis—the level of implementation observed.

Level of Implementation

We rated progress in an element using a straightforward scale, as follows:

0—Not Implementing. No evidence of the element.

1—Planning. The school was planning to or preparing to implement.

2—Piloting. The element was being partially implemented with only a small group of teachers or students involved.

3—Implementing. The majority of teachers were implementing the element, and the element was more fully developed in accordance with descriptions by the team.

4—Fulfilling. The element was evident across the school and was fully developed in accordance with the design teams' descriptions. Signs of institutionalization were evident.[1]

Examples of each of these follow.

Not Implementing. The school might have heard of it during training sessions, but was not working on it by either planning, preparation, or piloting.

Planning. Several teams require schools to develop teams that draw up plans in the first year for the implementation of elements in the following years. The school could be busy developing a technology-use plan or discussing different standards that might be adopted. We considered this level of activity as the introduction of an element or preparing the way for it. Alternatively, teachers might be in early discussions about how to develop new curriculum units, but had not actually developed the units or tried them in classrooms.

Piloting. Schools often began transition to a full multiyear student assignment by having two grades pilot it for a full year. Thus, only a few teachers are involved, but they are implementing. Alternatively, a group of teachers might have developed a single curriculum unit and were trying it out in classrooms. But not all teachers were participating in the effort, and only a few units had actually been developed and tested. Alternatively, all teachers might be piloting a unit, but it was a single unit per teacher that covered only a very small portion of the school day.

Implementing. All teachers might be using their newly developed curriculum units in their classes. A significant number of units (covering at least one-third of the curriculum over the course of the

---

[1]Implementation analysis often calls this level of implementation *institutionalizing* or *incorporating*, implying a level of stability and permanence. As the reader will discover in the rest of this report, our research indicates that the transience of the school and district political context often prevents institutionalization. We have thus used *fulfilling* to imply that the elements are present as the design teams intended, but we make no claim as to permanence.

year) must have been developed thus far.[2] Alternatively, a three was awarded when the computer technology the team described as necessary to the design was up and running in the classrooms, and teachers and children were experimenting using new pedagogy linked to the computers. In short, the infrastructure had to be there for all to use, and the pedagogical changes had to be grasped, but perhaps not fully developed.

Fulfilling. All appropriate teachers have adopted the practice and appear to have become "experts" themselves in the design. Signs of institutionalization and taking "ownership" are apparent. For example, schools have initiated their own internal quality checks that mimic the behavior of the design team in this regard. Schools have begun to train teachers from other schools in the design or have become demonstration sites for the design.

Application and Development of a Summary Dependent Variable

We initially applied these levels of implementation to each element that a design team intended to change in a school.[3] For *each element included in a design*, a score was given based on the observations and interviews conducted at the sites.[4]

---

[2]This proved to be particularly difficult to assign in the area of curriculum. How many units were enough to say that the implementing level had been accomplished? We arbitrarily said about a third of the curriculum. This would mean that a RW school would usually achieve an implementing-level score if the school had implemented the *Success for All* program within the two-year period. In this particular instance, we only assigned a three to a RW school if the school showed intention (committed to and put resources aside for) to adopt the remaining parts of the RW curriculum: World Lab and Math Wings.

[3]The reader should note that the use of numbers in the above scale does not imply interval-level data. The intervals between these points are not known. For example, a school with an average score of two is not half-way done with implementation. Neither is it twice as far along as a school scoring a one. The leap from planning to piloting might be far less formidable than the leap from implementation to the full vision of the design. In fact, a school scoring a three might take several more years to finish the design fully. The score indicates only what a school has accomplished in the way of implementation, as denoted in the above description.

[4]Reliability between raters was a potential issue in the creation of these scores. Reliability was increased by each rater performing this operation on a sample of schools that they and other raters had visited. The raters then exchanged scores and discussed discrepancies and how to resolve them.

We then developed an average score for each school to use as a summary variable. First, we summed across the elements of design identified for each design team. For the five common elements, we totaled the values for each element and then divided by five to arrive at a school implementation level.[5] No weighting was attached to particular elements. For assessment of more elements, we summed across those included in the design and divided by the appropriate number (from five to eight). We assigned schools to the above categorizations based on the average score.[6]

DIFFERENCES IN PROGRESS BY SCHOOLS

Over the two-year period of the scale-up phase, we tracked the progress made by schools toward their associated design team goals. The findings are summarized in Figures 4.1 and 4.2 using the five elements and the eight elements, respectively, and are encapsulated below:

- The data reveal significant variation in the progress made among the schools in the sample. The scores cover all the levels of implementation but cluster somewhat at the piloting and implementing levels.

- The difference between using five and eight elements is not significant at this level of aggregation.

- The differences among year 1 and year 2 schools are significant. Schools in their first year show lower levels of implementation than those in their second year of the initiative.

With some additional information about expectations for results, we placed a simple interpretation on these results. First, NAS's goal, agreed to by the teams, was for each team to have a three-year implementation strategy, meaning the design would be highly visible in the school and producing changes in student performance by the

---

[5]These five elements are curriculum, instruction, assessments, student groupings, and professional development.

[6]In assessing the total score of a school, the following intervals were used: A 0 or less than 0.8 was not implementing; a score equal to or greater than 0.8, but less than 1.6, was piloting, etc.

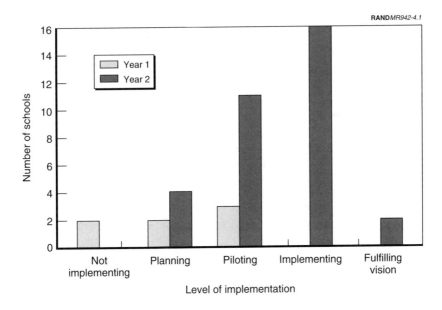

Figure 4.1—Implementation Levels Assessed at
Spring 1997: Five Elements

end of the third year of implementation. This does not mean that all teams believe their design would be fully developed and in place by the end of year three. Several believe that it will take longer to produce the full results and to reach fruition. Nevertheless, they did agree with NAS that a three-year schedule was appropriate for very significant portions of the design to be in place and for significant progress toward the full vision to be evident.

Second, and more important, this three-year implementation schedule was enforced by the district partners. These partners, faced in most instances with state assessments and new accountability mechanisms, felt the need to produce observable, measurable student improvements within three years. For example, some of the schools in Dade, Memphis, and San Antonio were the worst-performing schools in their respective states. As such, the states had issued policies that would allow state-level interventions if the schools' performances did not increase within three years. Several district representatives stated in interviews that, if results were not evident within that time, the designs would be abandoned.

Given this time line for expectations, we argue that a school would have to be at the "implementing" level for the five common elements by the end of the second year of implementation, or it would have difficulty meeting the vision of the design within three years, much less making significant improvement in student outcomes. In short, the elements of instruction, curriculum, appropriate assessments, effective student assignments, and new professional development approaches must be significantly in place (implementing or fulfilling level) by the end of the second year to say that implementation is proceeding quickly enough to meet the stated outcome time line of NAS, the teams, and the districts.

As Figure 4.1 shows, of the 33 year 2 schools in the sample, 18 (approximately 54 percent) are at the implementing level, and two are at the fulfilling level. However, 15 (close to 45 percent) are below this level, with four schools (12 percent) well below. These 15 schools are not likely to meet these goals without a significant

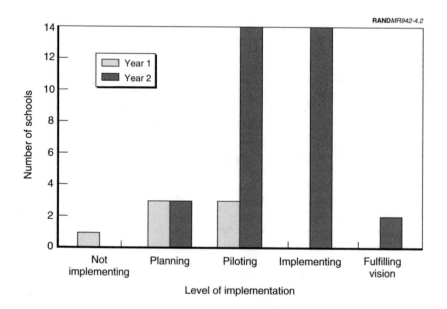

**Figure 4.2—Implementation Levels Assessed at
Spring 1997: Eight Elements**

increase in the pace of implementation. Meanwhile, of the seven year 1 schools in the sample, three (43 percent) are at least at the piloting phase, while two (29 percent) are not yet at the planning stage.

When all the elements that design teams chose to change are included (eight elements are used), the picture is about the same. Only 48 percent of the year 2 schools are implementing or fulfilling the vision of the design, while three are still planning. The year 1 schools again show three at least at the piloting phase.[7]

The remainder of this report illuminates these results by examining their relationship to four sets of factors: the selection process used by the school, design and team factors, school structural and site factors, and district and institutional factors.

---

[7]We note that several schools shift from one level to another when all eight elements are considered rather than just the five elements all design teams have in common.

Chapter Five

THE INFLUENCE OF THE SELECTION PROCESS AND SCHOOL CLIMATE

This chapter explores the relationship between the level of implementation observed and the efficacy of the match between design team and school. As shown in Figures 4.1 and 4.2, we found significant variation across schools. Part of this variation might be due to some "poor matches," in which the design fell on very infertile school ground. The fertility of the ground has three aspects: the general process of selection, the specific process of selection for a school, and the school receptivity or climate for reform.

This chapter examines the general picture of the matching process, setting the broad context. Important lessons can be drawn from this more-general assessment. Then the chapter focuses on each school's particular view of the selection process, examining the effects of two specific variables: the school staff's stated understanding of the design at the time of the selection and whether the staff had a choice among designs. Then the chapter focuses on conditions in the school at the time of the match and thereafter. Here, we are less concerned with the process and more concerned with the climate of support within the school. Thus, the analysis focuses on whether the school had existing tensions, whether the school had turnover in its leadership during the two-year effort, and preexisting reforms that might have sensitized the school to the design. The chapter ends with some implications about the selection process and continuity.

For these independent variables, each described below, we relied on the interview data for qualitative assessments of the value of the variables involved.

THE DISTRICT ROLE IN SELECTION

The districts played a significant role in the selection process and exercised important authority. In all cases,

- The district served as a gatekeeper in terms of selecting designs to be used in the district. While one district made it a policy to encourage the adoption of all the NAS designs, other districts ruled some designs inappropriate for their schools. In the case of NA, districts that had previously affiliated with that design used it exclusively in the first year of the scale-up, and only a handful of other design teams were working in NA districts at the time of this writing.[1]

- The districts decided which schools could participate. While several jurisdictions invited all or any school(s) to review the designs, two districts also targeted the matching—linking specific schools to specific design teams.

- District officials provided the organization for and infrastructure of the process that guided the selection of schools. Districts designated NAS coordinator(s) that were responsible for organization within the district and sometimes for each design team.

- Districts established an application process that often required school staff participation in the decision as evidence that the school was committed to implementing the design. Districts selected among applicants or brokered the agreement between an individual school and a design team.

The quick start had several implications for the matching process. First, districts and NAS had to establish the process at a time when school people were busy with testing regimes and when many staff had already determined how they would use their summer leave. Second, districts had to ask schools to make a major commitment at a time of the year when many of the planning and preparation activities for such an undertaking had already occurred. Schools had

---

[1]In previous documents, we have called the NA design a "systemic design," indicating that the team intended to work at the school, district, and state levels to bring about NA's vision of schooling. As such, it had already partnered with the two jurisdictions in our sample: Kentucky and Pittsburgh. Its relationships with these districts preceded the NAS scale-up phase. Thus, during the scale-up, these districts chose NA as a primary model for implementing school-level changes.

already developed school improvement plans, school budgets, Title 1 budgets, and special education programs for the coming year. Finally, rhetoric to the contrary, none of the designs had been proven at this point. Schools were being asked to make choices about designs based on limited data about the effectiveness of the designs in encouraging implementation in similar schools and based on limited data about the designs' ability to increase student performance.

The timing also affected the design teams. First, much of their attention was still focused on Phase 2 schools to meet the goal of a credibly demonstrated design by July 1995. NAS announced it was making a June 1995 decision on which design teams would continue into scale-up, and the ability to demonstrate the design was a key component of that decision.[2] The three years of design and demonstration phases had not provided sufficient time to develop the designs fully.[3] The first round of schools "shopping" for designs would buy designs still being developed. Second, as design teams were completing their demonstration work, they were tasked with developing marketing strategies and materials for scale-up. The more experienced teams, i.e., those that had marketed programs in the past, such as RW, had an advantage. Those who were still developing major elements of their designs or who suffered from leadership turnover or instability were at a disadvantage.[4]

DIFFERENCES AMONG DISTRICTS IN THE SELECTION PROCESS

Interviews and documents from all levels and all parties were used to piece together the differences in the matching process among districts and schools.

The districts associated with NAS each used slightly different processes to match design teams and schools. One set of districts (Dade, Memphis, and San Antonio) attempted to follow the process NAS had described, which included participation by all schools that were

---

[2]NAS did select seven of the nine demonstration teams to go on to scale-up. The decision reflected several factors that included the status of the demonstration schools.

[3]Bodily et al. (1996).

[4]This will be specifically covered in Chapter Six.

interested, information dissemination, design-team fairs, and a vote by schools as to which design to choose. Two other districts (Cincinnati and Philadelphia) did not use this process. They both targeted specific schools for initial implementation. In Cincinnati, a district-level panel guided the process and, with school input, gave final approval of each match. Philadelphia allowed a preselected group of schools choice among designs. The districts in Kentucky and Pittsburgh exclusively used the NA design, based on past district-level decisions. The schools we examined in these two districts had minimal exposure to other designs.[5] Finally, in most districts, some schools were idiosyncratically targeted. That is, even in districts that otherwise let schools choose, the district might have urged one or two schools to adopt a certain design.

In districts that promoted a choice among the designs, the most frequently used vehicle was the design fair, in which staff from each of the schools had an opportunity to attend design-team presentations, ask questions of the teams, and pick up materials. School staff in these districts reported this was the key event in the process, and the initial impression a team made at the fair was decisive in the school's willingness to consider a design. Many schools based their decisions solely on the fair and the materials at hand.

These fairs and initial materials from design teams received mixed reviews. Across the jurisdictions, district officials responsible for the process found that, while fairs provided one way to introduce the designs, they did not provide the depth of understanding and site-relevant details needed for informed decisionmaking. Many of the principals who attended these fairs agreed. One principal, for example, complained that the schools had made a major decision based on "thin information." The result, this respondent pointed out, was that his school latched onto a design that had a familiar component to it because that "seemed more concrete." More importantly, after the schools began actually implementing the design, a number of principals reported that their perception of the design, based on information gathered through the fair process, had been incomplete.

---

[5]Since the initial fairs in spring 1995, Pittsburgh has opened up the process to more designs, while Kentucky has recently made moves in this direction.

A second part of the decision process in some places was a visit by a small group from a school to a team's demonstration school to help the potential adoptor decide whether it wanted to partner with a design team. Principals who undertook this extra step identified visits to design-team demonstration sites as one of the most powerful ways to gain understanding of that design. Teachers who visited demonstration sites often commented that they could "visualize" the design better after the visit and that the visit made them more aware of "where we are going." In the latter case, this often meant that there was a greater sense of the design affecting the school as a whole, rather than just concentrating on a particular school program.

Unfortunately, in the initial selection process at the end of the demonstration phase, very few schools had the opportunity to send teams to demonstration sites. In part, this reflected the fact that the design teams had very few sites, often located at some distance from the jurisdiction. It also reflected the speed at which the first round of matching took place.

Concerns raised about visits to the demonstration sites occurred when school staff perceived that sites did not represent a schooling situation similar to their own. For example, inner-city schools sometimes had trouble identifying with EL demonstration schools in Dubuque, Iowa. Many visitors to CN's demonstration school worried that it was successful because it included a magnet program in a well-resourced environment.

Targeting Specific Schools for Designs

Districts using a more top-down approach to bring schools and design teams together depended to some extent on knowing whether a school was ready to consider restructuring and on knowing enough about the school to divine the best match. Design teams reported that they became frustrated with this approach because they wasted resources visiting schools that had little or no interest in pursuing the design. School staff in these instances said they were upset that design teams showed up at their door knowing little or nothing about the nature of that school.

However, there were some instances when targeted matchmaking reflected the demands of the design. For example, the AT design requires a pathway of schools, and district officials were key in getting the feeder pattern needed. In other instances, districts sought to build on existing resources and capacity. For example, districts sent the RW team to schools that were already using the *Success for All* reading component of the RW design, or sent the CN team to schools that already had extensive technology.[6]

With the targeted matching, many schools reported they felt pressured to adopt a design. Principals were aware that other designs existed, which they had no opportunity to review. In some cases, teachers reported feeling "railroaded," with little understanding of what they were agreeing to do.[7] Sometimes these ill feelings festered and affected the implementation, as will be discussed later.

Schools' Incentives to Adopt

Several themes emerged in school-level interviews about what incentives contributed to a school's decision to commit to a design, apply to adopt a design, or implement if the district had chosen the design for them.

First and foremost, schools reported adopting designs because they thought they would get access to outside resources, including professional development. All schools reported that they thought they would be adding either expertise or resources to their schools by adopting a design; however, the extent of resources and the types of resources varied by district. For example, principals in one district believed every school would receive $50,000 to support the implementation. In the Kentucky and Pittsburgh districts, schools that adopted the NA design were promised access to funding sources, such as Goals 2000 planning money or additional professional development days. These funds were not available if they did not adopt the design. In Pittsburgh, schools joining NA also were told they would gain significant control over most of their budgets and staffing. The schools reported joining for this reason. In Dade, a dis-

---

[6]The RW design has three curriculum components. *Success for All* is the language-arts component and predates NAS. Several hundred schools around the country are now using it.

[7]Teachers in one school related how the principal came to them individually during the summer and got them to sign off on the design. Few really knew what the design was or the full implications of their signature.

trict with site-based budgets, schools knew that joining involved the commitment of some of their own resources, but they also thought they would gain resources through the district payment for design-team services, computer technology, etc. In Dade and Cincinnati, schools reported they were expected to apply for grants to support some, but not all, of the implementation. The bottom line was that all schools reported that they expected some "additional resources" to flow to them when they adopted a design.

Secondly, they adopted designs because the "district was going in that direction." They chose to be early adopters because they "wanted to be out-front of the rest." In addition, the majority of the schools reported selecting designs because they thought the designs would help them build on what was already going on in the school. This often meant that school staff latched onto specific familiar aspects of the design, rather than viewing it holistically. No principals reported seeing this as an opportunity to change the school radically.

There were incentives against adopting designs. Across the schools, principals cited teacher concerns about the time demands and the unknown nature of the initiative. In secondary schools, there were complaints that most of the design teams did not appear to have either a very developed design or design team members familiar with the environment of secondary schools. In the end, schools in several districts chose not to adopt designs in the first two years for the above reasons or simply because of other commitments.

INFLUENCE OF THE SELECTION PROCESS

Our interviews with schools revealed that the selection process had important effects on implementation. In particular, schools that felt they had adopted a design without fully understanding it or that thought they were forced to adopt a design showed lower implementation.

Poor Understanding of the Design

Twelve schools reported that their choice of design was faulty or that they did not understand the design chosen for them. As compared to other schools, these 12 reported that, whether they chose the design or the design was chosen for them, they realized within a short time after they began implementing that the design did not suit their purposes or capabilities at all. This was most especially the case for two designs that required significant amounts of teacher development of curriculum and changes in organizational structures within the school. MR and AT each had four schools that responded in this manner. Presentations by design teams in the spring 1995 fairs or in other forums did not always convey clearly the nature of the design, and these two designs in particular appeared to be less well articulated.[8] After schools realized the extent of teacher time required to develop curriculum and instruction, they debated whether they should go forward. While valuable, this debate slowed the implementation effort. Our analysis shows a negative association between a poor initial understanding of the design and eventual implementation levels (see Figure 5.1).

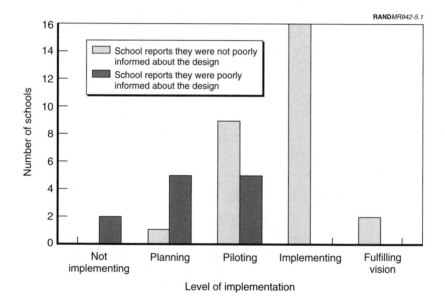

Figure 5.1—Level of Implementation of Poorly Informed Schools

---

[8]We will note later that this seemed to be connected to particular staff or leadership turnover in those two designs at the very period when presentations were being made.

Forced Choice of Design

Seven schools reported that they were "forced" by their districts to adopt a particular design. They overlap somewhat with those that say they did not understand the design well. Note that the issue is not whether or not schools had a choice of using design-based assistance. The issue is whether, given the school had to adopt a design, it could choose one it thought fit its circumstances. District respondents say they did not force a single school to accept the designs, with one exception.[9] But our interviews revealed that teachers and principals in at least seven schools reported that the central office made the choice for them. As some put it, "word came down from the central office that we were to adopt that design." In other cases, teachers reported that they voted but knew the vote had to go the way the central office wanted to go. They said they voted several times until "they got it right." Our analysis shows that schools that were forced to implement a design showed lower levels of implementation (see Figure 5.2).

INFLUENCE OF THE SCHOOL CLIMATE

Our analysis also showed that some designs did not fall on fertile ground for two reasons. First, some schools had preexisting tensions that prevented them from implementing the design. Second, some schools had leadership turnover. Both tended to result in lower levels of implementation.

Internal Tensions

All schools have internal tensions and politics at work. But it was clear that six schools in our sample faced *extreme* internal conflicts prior to accepting the design. The acceptance of the design did not ameliorate these conflicts and unify the school. Rather, the design choice fueled the conflicts. By *conflicts*, we mean that a significant number of teachers reported that the principal was "just waiting for retirement" and/or was not taking an active role in the leadership of the school. The teachers literally reported "hating the principal" and

---

[9]The exception is in Dade County, where the central office forced all schools on the state "probation" list to adopt the RW design in fall 1996.

thinking he or she was a "disgrace." Or other conflicts had divided the staff. This could be the result of a union action or favoritism on the part of a "ruling clique." In one case, the school had a magnet status, but the faculty was divided over what the "purpose" of the school was, with a large gulf existing between two parties and their beliefs. In another case, a member of the staff had been accused of and was being prosecuted for sexual harassment of students. This had divided the faculty into those who supported the accused and those who did not. Thus, the designs fell on "infertile soil," with school staffs' attention being directed elsewhere for the majority of the two years we examined.

Our analysis shows that those schools reporting these extreme internal tensions had lower levels of implementation (see Figure 5.3).

Leadership Turnover

Some schools reported a principal turnover within the two-year period we studied. As those familiar with schools know, this leader-

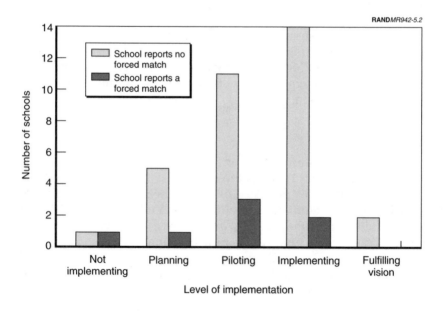

Figure 5.2—Level of Implementation of Schools with Forced Matches

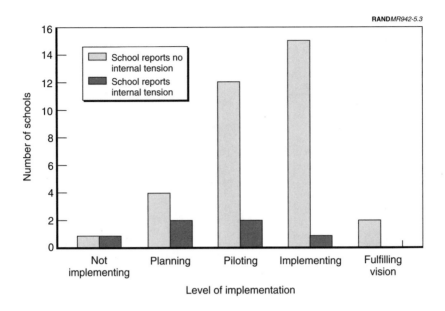

Figure 5.3—Level of Implementation of Schools with Internal Tensions

ship change often causes disruptions as the new management team is put in place. This simple disruption can slow down the implementation of a design. This can even be the case if the principal is a strong supporter of the design. It is even worse if the principal "was not on board." Within the sample, we found several instances of a new principal coming in who was "not on board"; rather, he or she was interested in pursuing his or her own vision of the school. But we also found several instances of school staff feeling the new leadership was a change for the better. Nevertheless, implementation slowed. Our analysis shows that schools reporting leadership turnover tended to have lower levels of implementation (see Figure 5.4).

Previous Reform Experiences

One factor that we believe might be very important, but lack the ability to properly analyze, is the extent to which schools were pre-

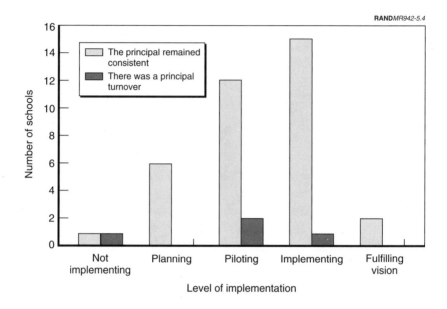

Figure 5.4—Level of Implementation of Schools with Principal Turnover

pared for implementation of a design by previous reform efforts. The picture is not clear because, in the sample, nearly all schools had some experience with reforms, but the schools varied significantly as to which reforms and the degree of their involvement. The picture is further obscured because each design might be more or less amenable to specific reforms. For example, MR and AT designs might be more easily implemented in schools that have a high level of participatory governance reforms in place. But the sample size and influences of other factors did not offer the ability to make that connection.

As an example, the sample contained two middle schools that had undertaken "middle school reforms." Both prided themselves on this. One of the schools took to its chosen design, seeing it as a furtherance of the reforms already undertaken. This school showed high levels of implementation. The other school did a pro forma implementation of the design. Teachers at the second school consistently reported that "we were already doing the design" under their middle school reform, even though they were not. They appeared to be content with the progress made in the past reform and were not looking for more depth.

INFLUENCE OF COMBINED EFFECT

Four of the above variables showed negative association with the level of implementation. However, as schools talked about these factors in interviews, it was clear that staff in some schools felt burdened by multiple factors and that the multiplicity of negative influences was important to the school staff's support for implementation.

Therefore, we took the sum of these four school-level factors for each school and determined whether, as a group, they were related to the level of implementation, (see Figure 5.5). The data indicate that, on average, the more of these issues a school had during the two years of the study, the lower its level of implementation. Alternatively, all the schools at the "implementing" or "fulfilling" levels have no more than one of these factors.

The single school in the sample with all these factors showed no visible implementation after one year. That school holds some lessons. Interviews with the principal and staff indicated that they respected the design-team members and appreciated the design. But as the principal put it, "We were not ready for this. We have other problems we must deal with first. In a year or two after things have settled down we might consider it." This gives a hint that there are some problems that design teams cannot address and that schools must have some "capacity or commitment" to make designs work. This might only be the willingness to undertake the design, but that is an important step. Without it, in inappropriate matches or in places of great turmoil, designs cannot make a difference in two years.

IMPLICATIONS AND LESSONS ALREADY LEARNED

All interviewees stated that the initial selection process in most districts was hurried and did not always proceed as planned. All schools were affected in some form or other by the timetable and the newness of the effort to all parties. This process was new to schools; they

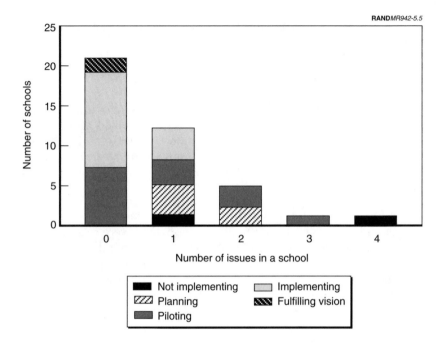

Figure 5.5—Issues Hindering Implementation

had little preparation for how to be "good consumers of design-based assistance." Our analysis showed that this process had some effect on implementation, depending on the specific process experienced by the school in question. Schools were likely to make more significant implementation progress within the two-year time frame we studied if they

- Were well informed about the designs

- Had a free choice among designs.

This finding has already been taken into account in improvements to the process. Many schools and districts provided feedback through different channels, including through RAND, on how to improve the effort. NAS has already drawn relevant lessons from its early experiences. Subsequent selection in these and other districts has changed:

- The process starts much earlier in the school year, giving schools more time to understand the design adequately and to prepare for implementation.

- While districts continue strong encouragement for schools to try design-based assistance in general, targeted matching is strongly discouraged in favor of schools having an open choice among the designs.

- In continuing districts in which many schools are already demonstrating the design, prospective school staff have opportunities to visit the demonstration sites and talk with implementing school staff.

- Districts, NAS, and the design teams provide schools with much more information during the selection process on both the short- and long-term resource commitments the school requires.

The bottom line is that the selection process we witnessed and that affected the first two years of scale-up implementation has already been changed to probably improve it. But our findings still hold for the schools in this sample.

The findings about the influence of school climate deserve attention. Our analysis shows that schools are more likely to show higher levels of implementation if they

- Did not have significant internal strife prior to undertaking the design

- Did not have leadership turnover during the two years studied.

Perhaps different expectations are needed for schools in strife or more effective strategies are needed for dealing with these situations. During the two years studied, design teams appeared to enable schools to deal with many problems, but they had difficulty overcoming preexisting divisions among staff or maintaining steady progress when a change in leadership occurred.

In summary, some schools appeared to be fertile ground for this type of reform, while others were not. Differences among schools indicate that the ground can be made fertile by previous training experiences, better preparation of the schools about what to expect from design teams, better preparation by design teams to deal with internal issues, more-sensitive policies for leadership change on the part of the district, and perhaps some design-team strategies for dealing with leadership transition.

All of this hints that the school support for a design is tenuous. It takes care and maintenance and clarity of communication among the parties involved. The findings indicate that the care, maintenance, and clarity must begin earlier rather than later.

Chapter Six

INFLUENCE OF DESIGN AND TEAM FACTORS

In this chapter, we turn to design and team factors to understand how they affected implementation. We first display the level of implementation of the schools by design team. We then sort through different design and team factors to understand their association with the level of implementation. The factors we examined were the stability of the team itself and its ability to grow, the ability of the teams to market themselves effectively to schools, the ability of the teams to market themselves effectively to districts, the approach to implementation taken by the teams, and the types of assistance provided by teams. The first factor—the stability of the team and its ability to grow—had ripple effects throughout implementation, so we address this issue first.

We also caveat this analysis heavily. The number of observations for each team is limited, especially when we control for the district-level influences we describe later. Thus, in several cases, the sample might unfairly represent the progress made by some teams, as noted below. Nevertheless, we believe the analysis provides some provocative insights of value.

LEVEL OF IMPLEMENTATION BY DESIGN TEAM

The level of implementation varied significantly by schools when sorted by design team. Figures 6.1, 6.2, and 6.3 show this relationship using the percentage of schools at each level of implementation for each design team. The pattern of level of implementation by design team held generally true when sorted in several different ways—by year 1 and year 2 schools or by five or eight elements. The findings are straightforward:

- RW and EL show higher levels of implementation than the other teams. This is due in part to the fact that RW deals only with elementary schools, and elementary schools fare better than other grade levels in our sample (see Chapter Seven). EL does fairly well in implementing its design in all schools. It appears to do better in secondary schools than other teams (i.e., its average score goes down when only elementary schools are considered).

- AT, MR, and NA show lower levels of implementation than other teams, with some variation for AT depending on which schools are included in the analysis. These lower scores might be affected by the particular sample we chose. Three of the seven NA schools are in Pittsburgh, and three of the five AT schools are in Philadelphia. In Chapter Eight, we will show that school staff reported these to be the least supportive districts during the period studied. Thus, the implementation levels of these teams might

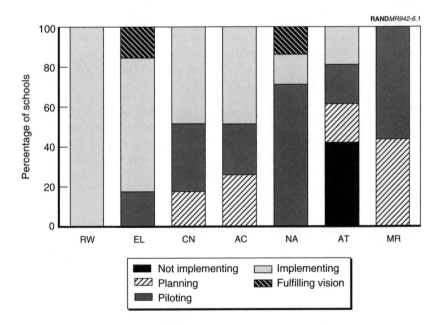

Figure 6.1—Design Team Levels of Implementation: Five Elements

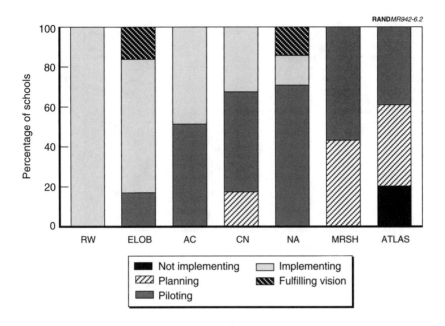

Figure 6.2—Design Team Levels of Implementation: Eight Elements

be unduly affected by the districts in which they worked. Finally, the MR year two schools in Dade and Memphis fared less well than the MR year one schools in San Antonio, implying that the initial strategy of MR or those districts might have influenced the results.

- AC and CN fall somewhere in the middle, depending on which grade levels and elements are considered.

DESIGN AND TEAM FACTORS AND THEIR INTERRELATIONSHIP

Our analysis here depends strongly on interview data from the schools and districts and design teams, as well as on a review of materials provided by designs. In developing these variables, we relied on our work in the demonstration phase to develop specific questions and also used a more open-ended approach—letting the

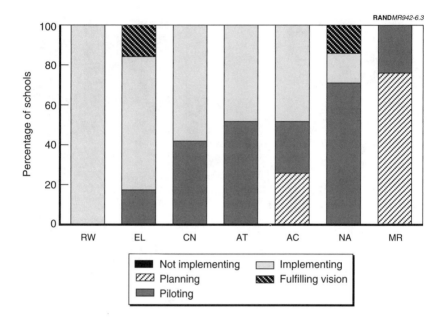

**Figure 6.3—Design Team Levels of Implementation in
Year 2 Schools: Five Elements**

respondents indicate what was important to them in terms of
design-team support of their implementation and in terms of the
design teams' ability to provide that support. We coded the value of
the factor using *weak, medium,* or *strong,* as applicable.

Our analysis of the data indicates that no one or two design and team
factors explain the dependent variable. Thus, we will not show the
dependent variable arrayed against each of the independent variables in separate figures as in the previous chapter. Rather, our
interviews revealed a complex series of variables at work that *jointly
added to strong effects,* as reported by schools.

Our interviews showed that some factors that schools had not identified or only indirectly identified had strong effects. The level of
support that a design team provided to schools depended on the
negotiation that took place between the district and the design team.
It also depended on the capabilities and stability of the team itself. A

school might not have been aware of these influences but was aware of what types of support were provided and the type of design undertaken. Thus, we have a stew of factors that are important for understanding the influences on implementation: design-team capabilities, district–design team negotiations, the design itself, and the actual type of support provided. Finally, we cannot forget that some teams did not communicate their designs very well, and this had an influence. While the last factor has been covered before from the schools' perspective, here it appears again as a "design team" factor with explanations of why there were differences among designs.

Our understanding of the importance of these factors among teams is summarized in Figure 6.4, with the design teams aligned roughly in groups by their relative implementation levels, as determined by review of different measures of the dependent variable. The simple pattern shows that the following were important contributors to design implementation within the two-year time of our study:

• **A stable team with a capability to serve.** Several factors were taken into account, including lack of major staff or leadership upheavals or loss of important staff, reported numbers of "on-site" field staff and numbers of visits to schools during the two-

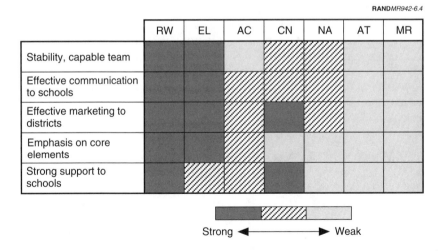

Figure 6.4—Design Team Factors Related to Implementation

year period, reports from schools about the general competency of the design-team staff, and reports from schools about the ability of the team to respond to their queries when contacted.

- **Ability to communicate the design well to schools.** This assessment primarily relied on schools' and districts' statements about the efficacy of the early descriptions of the designs through printed materials or through interactions with the teams. It helps explain why some design teams had more difficulty getting and maintaining support within schools.

- **Effective marketing to the district and ability to gain needed resources for implementation.** This assessment took into account the district's views of the relationship with the team and the ability of each team to garner the professional development days and other resources from the district needed for implementation.

- **Type of design or relative elements emphasized.** Each design emphasizes particular elements. This was found to be important to implementation in the demonstration phase and was tracked here as well.

- **Implementation support to schools.** This assessment was based on the types of support provided. Some designs were judged by schools and district to have provided stronger support. Others were criticized for the lack of support. Strong support appeared to be associated with the provision of whole-school training, extensive professional-development days, and facilitators.

Each of these is covered in turn below, drawing out the interrelationships involved to create a whole picture of design and team influence.

TEAM STABILITY AND CAPABILITY TO SERVE

We return here to one of the inherent tensions within the NAS strategy. During the period studied, the teams were required to evolve from small, often research-oriented organizations into entrepreneurial enterprises. They were expected to serve more schools at the same time that they were expected to deliver quality—sound implementation and student outcomes. At the same time, their resources from NAS made up a decreasing portion of their operating revenues. Three teams appeared to have a particularly difficult set of circumstances in this regard: AC, AT, and MR.

AC has always been the smallest of the teams, with a comparatively slim field structure and headed by a very strong leader—Audrey Cohen. In 1996, the team faced two crises: Its single national facilitator, a former principal in an AC school, retired from the organization. Then, Audrey Cohen passed away. Understandably, the team's support to schools during this period waned. Schools reported a gap in the level of support in the second year of scale-up. Part of this gap was the lack of implementation checks and the lack of training for new teachers. Schools did not receive the level of feedback they thought they needed to continue at this vital juncture. And schools with high mobility rates, like those in Dade, did not receive the training for new staff that was needed to pursue the design more fully.

AT started the scale-up phase in a difficult position. From the beginning, this design team has both benefited and suffered from having to blend the thoughts and ideas of its four founders into a coherent and implementable design. A lack of coherence and coordination among the founding organizations had contributed to slow implementation in the demonstration phase. At the end of the demonstration phase, the project director stepped down. Scale-up began with a director new to the project and with unresolved internal funding and staffing issues among the four parent organizations. It is no wonder that, in the first year of the scale-up phase, school staff complained of poor explanations by the design team and lack of support. Some schools have never recovered from the initial confusion in the early days of scale-up.

MR also suffered from team growing pains during this period. It had developed its design during demonstration with a heavy reliance on consultants. As it sought to become self-supporting, it decided to develop a more permanent staff and resolve internal issues with its parent organization, the Hudson Institute. During scale-up, it had to build a staff to explain and deliver the design. It had a year-long period of what could be described as a shakedown as it tried to acquire and train staff to support its sites, while trying to determine in the midst of reorganization what the costs and prices of the design would be. This included the departure from the team of the associate director—a person schools stated they admired and felt "communicated well" with them.

Schools entering into partnership at this time complained of poor explanations of the design. Districts complained of poor cost estimation that required revisiting the contracts and contributed to tensions between the design team and its districts. Again, early confusion was hard to overcome. Within our sample, schools that entered into partnerships with MR in the second year exhibited much less confusion and stronger implementation.

ABILITY TO COMMUNICATE THE DESIGN WELL TO SCHOOLS

In our interviews, the schools talked in very different terms about the design teams and how well they communicated their ideas to schools.

We noted in Chapter Five that respondents in 12 schools in the sample showed some consensus that they did not fully understand the design when they chose it—they had been poorly informed. We also noted that four of these schools were associated with AT and another four with MR. In particular, schools were often confused over or surprised by what they would be called upon to do to implement the designs. In several cases, this led to a year of haggling over what would be done or a year of not doing much of anything while the school tried to figure out if it was going to go ahead. We have already explained why these two designs in particular suffered from this problem.

The contrast with RW and EL is marked. RW grew from a team and reading program that has been in existence for some time. School-level personnel often know about the *Success for All* reading component of the design before hearing about the full RW design. *Success for All* has been well-communicated in journals and the press. RW, after many years in this business, has extensive materials that can be provided to schools to explain the design. While EL has nowhere near this level of sophistication in marketing, it too has an important name association: Outward Bound. It also can communicate the design fairly easily through its materials and through its ten "principles." Both use school-level personnel from existing design-based schools in their marketing to explain the design. Finally, we must add that school personnel often told us that the EL team appeared to be "one they felt they could work with" or that team members were "helpful, respectful, and listened to their needs." Nevertheless, the team was criticized for not having convincing demonstration sites.

CN's ability to communicate its design to schools also stands apart. While it did not perform particularly well from the point of view of most schools in terms of communicating the details of the design, it was consistently listed as the number one or two choice of most schools. This is because it has labeled itself or gotten labeled as the "high tech" design. All schools would like to be on the leading edge of technology, and this design promises to help schools acquire and use technology effectively. As such, it has received keen interest from most schools.

The simple message from this is that marketing to schools is an important part of implementation and that poor starts might be avoided through better marketing.

EFFECTIVE MARKETING TO THE DISTRICT AND ABILITY TO GAIN NEEDED RESOURCES FOR IMPLEMENTATION

The teams also had to market themselves to the districts and gain the districts' verbal and funding support for professional development and other activities. This marketing was very important because districts controlled the majority of funds that were to be used for implementation. But it was also important for the districts because they were committing to the transformation of multiple schools using particular designs. What was negotiated between a design team and a district would apply to more than one school. Thus, the districts took the negotiations seriously.

The teams used many different marketing approaches, and district staff and design teams report that some were more effective than others in gaining district support and approval. Several comparisons should suffice to get at some of the differences.

RW had a fairly straightforward approach when it came to marketing to districts. It targeted Title 1 funds for implementing the design—

discretionary funds for at-risk student populations available for whole-school programs.[1]   It had a package of materials that explained how the design could be funded. Because of the high demand for its design, the team presented funding options clearly and discouraged negotiations over customized packages of services. Districts reported that they knew what they were getting and what they could and could not negotiate. Importantly, districts could not negotiate the amount of training needed or its form. The district either agreed to a package or did not—and the package had been developed over several years through experience to ensure a level of funding that would promote implementation.

In contrast, other teams did not target this funding stream for implementation and did not have the same level of marketing experience as the RW design team. The demonstration phase had given most teams little information regarding the cost of implementation. Even if it had, conditions were changed enough with the scale-up strategy that this information might not apply. Thus, most other teams entered comparatively extensive negotiations over what level and types of training would be provided. To its credit, EL quickly learned the pitfalls of this approach and began to solidify its options and areas of negotiation.

While the CN design did require extensive negotiation, it quickly found a special niche to claim in district negotiations that worked to its benefit. CN requires significant computer and telecommunication technologies in the school to be successful; in the words of the team, the technology must be ubiquitous. This is quite expensive for most schools and districts and could therefore form a stumbling block in negotiations over funding. However, CN marketed itself as a "demonstration program for learning technologies." The team convinced districts to use the design in several schools as the means to learn about and demonstrate the use of technology to other schools. This approach appeared to work in each of the districts in which we sampled CN schools. Those schools were allocated a significant portion of the district's technology acquisition funds, technology staff positions, etc., to make the design work. While districts all think of

---

[1]Title 1 is a federal program that provides funding to schools to help educate "at-risk" children. Many NAS schools received significant amounts of this funding.

CN as an expensive design because of the needed technology, they have been willing to cover the costs in a few schools with the understanding that these schools will be test beds for emerging technology.

In contrast, the AT and MR designs asked not only for fees but for significant governance changes up front. This required more strenuous negotiations with districts simply because the designs require considerable school-level autonomy to implement. For example, the AT design requires the creation of a semiautonomous feeder pattern of elementary schools, middle schools, and a high school in a contiguous geographic area. Interlocking teams of teachers within this "pathway" form the basis of decisionmaking for the rest of the design. This pathway construct is difficult to achieve and requires prolonged conversations among the parties (teams, district, and schools) to set up. But without these changes, several important implementation steps, such as the review of standards and curriculum across the pathway for one, cannot occur. If this pathway concept takes a long time to set up and begin functioning, all the other elements of the design are stalled in implementation as a practical matter.

Likewise, MR required significant autonomy be granted to the school and, like CN, required significant technology and software to be acquired and used in its schools. It did not use the approach CN used to sell the technology component to the district. MR often became bogged down in discussions over levels of decentralization and funding for technology. In general, districts did not provide the funding to acquire the needed technology. As a result, during the course of this study, elements of its design were slow to appear, especially those in the instructional element that require technology support for individual education compacts and learning.

Just as importantly, the results of the resource negotiations varied dramatically from district to district for some teams. For example, EL asked for and got 12 to 13 days of professional development per teacher in the three districts we sampled. RW got a lesser amount, but one consistent across districts. In contrast, the MR negotiations resulted in about three days in Dade, seven days in Memphis, nine days in San Antonio, and about four in Philadelphia.

In short, design-team negotiations with districts had an important influence on allocated resources and eventually on implementation.

Some design teams failed to get a consistent level of professional development days. We infer that some teams appear to have found more fruitful marketing and negotiation approaches with districts than others.

TYPE OF DESIGN OR RELATIVE ELEMENTS EMPHASIZED

The design teams do focus on different design elements; therefore, they approach implementation differently. We refer the reader back to our original work in describing the teams.[2] In this work, we noted that several teams (AC, CN, EL, and RW) appeared to focus on what we called the core elements of schooling: curriculum, instruction, student assignment, student assessment and professional development. Other teams (AT, MR, and NA) had included more elements, such as standards, school and district governance, public involvement, and integrated social services. We called these comprehensive and systemic designs. Their approaches to implementation emphasized a focus on the supportive connections to district, home, and community to build collaboration and internal capacity to sustain the reform over time.

In the demonstration phase, we found that these comprehensive and systemic designs, as we called them, made less progress toward their own goals for school-level implementation within the two years studied. There were at least three reasons for this: First, these designs attempted to change a greater number of elements; they took on a greater implementation task with the same time constraints as others. Second, some of those elements proved very difficult to change because of the extensive interaction needed by many parties not under the control of the team. Governance and integrated social services were two such elements. Finally, their approaches to implementation emphasized the changing of these additional elements first in an attempt to build collaboration and capability for self-transformation at the school level. For example, all three teams require the setting up of school-level teams to discuss existing performance gaps, possible remedies, and the creation of plans, before the implementation of other elements. If these prior steps are slow

---

[2]Bodilly et al. (1996).

to build or do not coalesce, the implementation of the other elements is delayed.

This finding should also hold true for the scale-up phase. To get at this issue, we took a different look at the data. We took the average score for each school on the five core elements and the average score on the three other elements. For each school, we looked for the highest score and inferred from it that the design either focused on the five core elements (equivalent to the common elements), the three other elements, or implemented all elements equally, as shown in Table 6.1.

Two designs (EL and RW) kept their emphasis on the five core (now common) elements, getting curriculum, instruction, and student assignment practices in place. Both did so quite consistently and successfully across the schools we sampled. Two other teams (AC and CN) put equal emphasis on the five core elements and the other elements included in their designs, in this case, public engagement for AC and the benchmarking process for CN. These teams were somewhat less successful in getting implementation across the board.

As with the demonstration phase, the comprehensive or systemic teams (AT, MR, and NA) continued to focus in the first year of implementation more on the non-core elements as the entry point to

Table 6.1

Relative Emphasis of Each Team During Implementation

		Number of Schools Emphasizing			
	Number of Schools	Five Core Elements	Three Comprehensive Elements	All Elements Equally	Relative Implementation Emphasis
RW	5	3	1	1	Core
EL	6	6	0	0	Core
AC	4	1	1	2	All
CN	6	2	3	1	All
NA	7	1	6	0	Comprehensive
AT	5	1	4	0	Comprehensive
MR	7	0	7	0	Comprehensive

design implementation. In particular, each of these designs required or strongly encouraged

- the building of participatory teams within the school to review past performance

- the review of standards for graduation, beginning public engagement

- development of *plans* for changes to the other elements of the design (curriculum, instruction, technology, etc.).

For these three designs, the preliminary efforts are intended to set the stage for stronger curriculum and instructional practices later and for building a capacity within the school for continued self-improvement. It is no wonder that many schools associated with these designs are in planning and piloting phases at their second year of implementation—the first full year of implementation is largely taken up with planning the implementation of many of the elements. This more planning-driven approach takes more time to set up. If not implemented well, further progress on other elements of the designs is delayed. For example, a school failing to set up effective governing teams in the AT design cannot take any of the other steps in the design.

These results hint at, but are not conclusive of, an important difference among teams. Focusing on the core elements has high initial payoff in getting teachers to implement the design. Focusing on other areas as the means of entering into discussions of how to change the core elements might help set the stage for later important changes and for self-improvement. But it also presents initial implementation barriers that take time to overcome and that have a domino effect on the implementation of other elements.

The data so far do not give an indication of which is the better approach in the long run. We emphasize that, in the short run (two years), the approach of the more-comprehensive teams still appears to go more slowly than the approach of the core-focused teams.

Our sample does show a unique coupling of core and comprehensive designs that produced strong implementation results. Two NA schools in Kentucky—one in this sample, the other in the demonstration phase sample—adopted both the NA design and a very specific curriculum and instructional package. One school chose Montessori, another chose the Galef Institute's Different Ways of Knowing. In both phases, these two schools showed high levels of implementation. In addition, both schools have shown significant gains in the KIRIS assessment system, and the Kentucky Department of Education has recognized them as exemplary demonstration sites. Thus, the systemic design of NA, which includes a focus on the governance and social service structures surrounding a school, can be effectively combined with another design that focuses primarily on curriculum and instruction to produce a more comprehensive implementation.

DESIGN-TEAM SUPPORT

The design teams' direct support to schools can have several components: materials, training, use of facilitators, design-team visits other than training, and the use of planning time within the schools. Each team put different emphasis on these supports (see Figure 6.5). Within this chart, the design teams are arranged by their level of implementation.

First, if a design team's presence on an everyday basis is important in the schools as many teachers and principals stated, some teams did a better job of ensuring this than others. Both RW and AC call for the creation of positions in the school, filled by school personnel, whose job is to help facilitate the design in the school. This appears to have some payoff. Similar in notion, each San Antonio school had a full time "instructional guide" as part of the district's support. This guide became something like a design-team facilitator within each school. Schools, teams, and district-level staff attribute the smooth implementation in San Antonio at least in part to the existence of the guides. Indeed, the MR design appeared to take off in these San Antonio schools, although it had difficulties in other districts. This was due in part to better explanations by the team during the selection process, in part to better relations with the district, and in part to this school-level presence.

Whole-staff immersion into the design also appears to pay off. The designs using this method made more progress on implementation according to our scale, which scores higher as more teachers

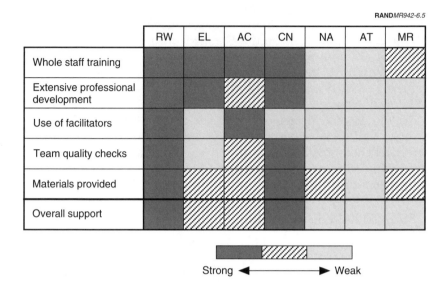

Figure 6.5—Implementation Interventions Emphasized by Teams

implement the design. As we found in the demonstration phase, the lead-teacher training approach often limited the design implementation to a few teachers within the school or created tensions within the school. In one case, after an initial year of very slow implementation, the district asked the AT design to abandon its lead-teacher model of training and train the whole staff. The second year began with a significantly increased group of teachers being exposed to the design through training. By the end of the year, the school showed large improvements in implementation. Another district is now considering the same request to AT to ensure more depth of implementation.

Design-team visits and implementation checks were important in teachers' eyes to ensure that they were making needed progress and to ensure that they had feedback. Two teams appear to have implemented these checks quite successfully from the point of view of the school and district staff.

The CN design calls for "critical friends" visits among their schools. After some design-team training for this purpose, a team of teachers from several different schools visited a targeted school essentially to perform an implementation audit. These visits can take a single day or can last up to a week. At the end of the visit, the visiting team presents its findings to the receiving school. The receiving school must review these findings and present a plan on how to address them. The staff who have visited schools have found this process to be an important professional development activity for themselves, while the staff at receiving schools have taken the findings of "their peers" very seriously. District personnel attest to the thoughtfulness and seriousness of the process. This process offers a means of checking implementation levels at schools, a means for professional development, and a mechanism for collegial interaction and sharing on topics of mutual importance.

In contrast, the RW design has formulated an "implementation check" that is just as well-received. It, however, is performed by trained RW staff who formally visit the school and provide a written report to the school on implementation issues. The school staff stated they found this very valuable and took the recommendations seriously, often using the recommendations to identify needed professional development for the next year.

Our data do not allow us to draw firm lessons in regard to the best package of supports to offer. For example, EL has exhibited strong implementation but lacked some of the supports other teams offered. It focused on extensive whole-school and individual training, as compared to other teams. This approach appears to work for them.

Finally, design teams often did not meet their own goals for an implementation strategy because of the failure to market themselves well within a district or because of reduced internal capability. This failure to follow their own strategy, for whatever reason, often accounted for poor implementation results in particular schools. For example, the AC design team did not stringently require a full-time facilitator in all schools. In the second year of implementation, the team failed to perform its own prescribed implementation checks, at least according to sources at schools. Thus, its "presence" in schools waned considerably in the second year—leading to lower visible levels of implementation and to teacher concerns.

IMPLICATIONS

NAS's intention was to ensure that teams developed into self-sufficient enterprises that could both assist high-quality implementation in schools and assist many schools simultaneously. Our observations revealed that the designs varied in their abilities and capabilities over this period and that a good part of this variability has to do with the designs themselves and their approaches to implementation. But another part has to do with the teams' ability to transform themselves from design teams into enterprises—to sell themselves and to price well in a growing market for whole-school reform. Higher levels of implementation were associated with design teams that

- Had a stable team with the capacity to field qualified personnel to serve growing numbers of schools

- Effectively communicated their designs to schools and avoided school staff confusion

- Effectively marketed to districts and gained the resource support required for the design

- Emphasized the core elements of schooling common across the designs: curriculum, instructions, student assignment, assessments, and professional development

- Supported implementation with whole-school training, facilitators, extensive training days, quality checks, and materials.

Clearly, an important part of the story of NAS revolves around the issue of whether the teams could produce high-quality "break-the-mold designs" at the same time they were becoming self-sufficient and were dealing with multiple districts and increasing numbers of schools in scale-up. Teams in certain instances offered less-than-high quality and had to make concessions on innovative ideas to "gain quantity." All the NAS teams ended this two-year period stretched more than when they entered. But all ended with many lessons learned and proposals for how to improve the delivery of their services. Importantly, all had charged for their services and found takers. All became more knowledgeable as to what they could actually offer in scale-up and what it would cost.

Becoming an enterprise proved stressful for all teams. Several design-team representatives have stated that going to a fee-for-service basis was both the best and worst thing that could have happened to them during this period. They have said it was beneficial because it pushed them away from philosophical positions toward real products that consumers could use and judge for effectiveness. It forced them to face a real market. They also have said it was difficult because, to gain partners, they had to review their thinking, products, and ideas all over again. Some were forced to make important changes that they hope will prove beneficial in the long run.

Chapter Seven

INFLUENCE OF SCHOOL STRUCTURAL AND SITE FACTORS

This chapter reviews the influence of school structural and site factors on the level of implementation. Specifically, we review the effects on implementation of the grade level served, the poverty level of the school's students, teacher mobility, and student-teacher ratios. For this analysis, we rely primarily on district and school documents that straightforwardly describe the schools' characteristics.

GRADE LEVEL INFLUENCE ON LEVEL OF IMPLEMENTATION

A long line of research points to significant differences in implementation of reforms associated with the grade level of the school.[1] In general, elementary schools are thought to be more likely to adopt and implement reforms, while middle schools and high schools are thought to be more resistant to reform.

The literature provides many reasons for the greater resistance to reform by middle and high schools. These include the size of the schools relative to elementary schools; the ingrained departmental structure, which prevents interdepartmental collaboration and encourages specialization; and the influence of and need to emulate the curriculum and structure of colleges and universities.

We found that NAS schools' implementation levels showed the expected pattern when sorted by the grade level of the school (see

---

[1]Bidwell (1996), Newman (1996), Sebring (1995), and Sizer (1992).

Figures 7.1 and 7.2). For year 2 schools, 66 percent of elementary schools were at the implementation or fulfilling level for the five elements, compared to only 33 percent of the middle and high schools. This ratio remained the same for middle and high schools when using the eight elements. Elementary schools showed less implementation with the eight-element list, with only 57 percent at the implementation or fulfilling level.[2]

One middle school and one high school in our sample were the exceptions to the rule, having fairly high levels of implementation. These two schools had quite different structures than those of

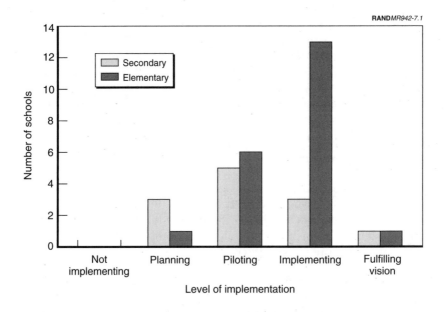

RAND*MR942-7.1*

Figure 7.1—Implementation Level by Grade Level Served:
Year 2 Schools with Five Elements

---

[2]We note that there is a high correlation between grade level served and size of the school. We examined enrollment level and its effect on implementation level and found a similar relationship to that described for grade level. We also found a disconfirming fact: One or two elementary schools with unusually high enrollments showed strong implementation.

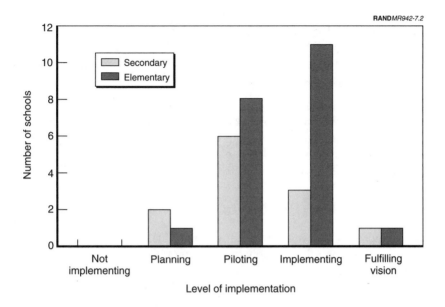

**Figure 7.2—Implementation Level By Grade Level Served:
Year 2 Schools with Eight Elements**

"typical" secondary schools in the sample. For example, they were much smaller; the high school was considered an "alternative" high school; and both had largely dropped the departmental structure before the NAS engagement.

In short, our findings are consistent with those of others who found that secondary schools are difficult to engage in reform and restructuring.[3] Even the two secondary schools in our sample that showed high levels of implementation lend support to the reasons secondary schools are so difficult to change. We would, however, add another major reason for the poor showing of implementation in secondary schools.

In developing and implementing their designs, the design teams tended to focus first on elementary schools. Thus, the designs are

---

[3]Bidwell (1996), Newman (1996), Sebring (1995), and Sizer (1992).

more complete and the implementation experiences are fuller at the elementary level than at the secondary level. At the time of this study, the design teams simply did not have the experience or the full designs needed to provide design-based assistance to high schools and middle schools.

This statement is based not just on our reading of the designs but on the testimony of school and district personnel, who consistently noted that the designs seemed less developed for the higher grades and that the teams seemed less experienced with the implementation demands of these grade levels.

INFLUENCE OF OTHER SCHOOL SITE FACTORS

We collected data on other independent variables associated with the school that would be likely to have an effect on the implementation outcomes. These included the socioeconomic level of the school, the level of teacher mobility, and the student-teacher ratio. In general, we found less clear relationships with the dependent variable but did find instances in specific schools where these factors proved to be important. Each of these is discussed briefly below.

Poverty Level of the School

Some might think that the ability to implement a design would be linked to the challenge inherent in the school population itself. That is, schools serving more needy populations would require more time to implement and have more difficulty doing so.

To test this, we used a simple indicator of the percentage of students in the school who received free and reduced-price lunches and plotted it against the implementation level of the school. This resulted in a typical "shotgun" scatter plot with no discernible pattern or trend.

Other student demographics could have been included, but they were not evident in our sample. For example, a large shift in the characteristics of the student population might stress a school making it impossible both to implement a new design and to deal with the student changes at the same time. The schools in our sample did not report such sudden shifts.

Teacher Mobility

We note one other important factor that we did not capture consistently—teacher mobility. Several schools in the sample experienced significant turnover in the implementation period. This was routine for the districts and schools involved and was not due to the design-team association as far as we could tell. However, it fell to the design team to train and retrain the constantly changing staff. If this was done well, the implementation went forward. In one or two cases where this training of new staff had not taken place, the implementation suffered. In one school, by the end of the year 2, one-third of the staff lacked design-team training because of turnover. This school could not be said to be implementing the design well.

This issue focuses on the overlap between school factors and design and team factors. In schools with high mobility in the teacher population the specific training regime of the team became even more important.

Student-Teacher Ratio

Finally, we examined the student-teacher ratio and its association with implementation. Our analysis showed a negative association—the greater the average number of students per teacher in the class, the lower the level of observed implementation. However, examination of the data on students in classes caused us to question the relationship. Each jurisdiction used different definitions of class size or counted different types of teachers when determining this ratio, and each had changed definitions over time. Also, data the schools reported and data the jurisdiction reported did not match. This possible relationship deserves more scrutiny, but we could not examine it further within the confines of this study.

IMPLICATIONS

Our review confirmed a general finding of the literature on school reform: that implementation tends to be slower in the secondary grades than in the elementary grades. Stronger progress was made in alternative or restructured secondary schools than in "typically" structured secondary schools.

Interviews with districts, design teams, and schools indicated that the design teams' efforts in developing the designs for the higher grade levels were not as strong as for the elementary levels. The teams appeared to be less prepared to deal with the unique difficulties of overcoming the resistance of secondary school structures but made significant progress when those structures had already been dismantled. Interviews also indicated that appropriate implementation interventions by design teams might have contributed to this result.

This clearly implies that the work of the teams and NAS is not done. Our findings show that further development of the designs and specific interventions and strategies for the higher grades are needed.

Chapter Eight

INFLUENCE OF JURISDICTIONAL AND INSTITUTIONAL FACTORS

In Chapter Four, we indicated that the level of implementation varied by school. Some of this variation has been accounted for by the selection process, school climate, design and team influence, and school structure. Here, we turn to the influence of the jurisdiction and institutional factors. This chapter first describes the level of implementation across districts. Next, it examines the relationships between different district and institutional factors and the level of implementation. The factors examined are leadership support and centrality of the effort, the existence of a crisis, the existence of a culture of cooperation and trust between the district and the schools, the level of autonomy provided to schools, the level of resource support provided and where funds came from, and the effects of specific assessments and accountability packages. Finally, we discuss some implications of district-level support for further efforts.

DISTRICT AND INSTITUTIONAL INFLUENCE ON LEVEL OF IMPLEMENTATION

The level of implementation varied significantly across districts. This variation changed when different subsets of the sample were used: five elements, eight elements, year 1 schools, or year 2 schools. However, across these different breakdowns of the dependent variable, there was some general consistency in that districts sorted into two clusters. These findings are displayed in Figures 8.1 through 8.4, which provide the percentage of schools at different implementation levels for five and eight elements and for year 2 schools only. As in previous discussions, the distinction between year 1 and year 2

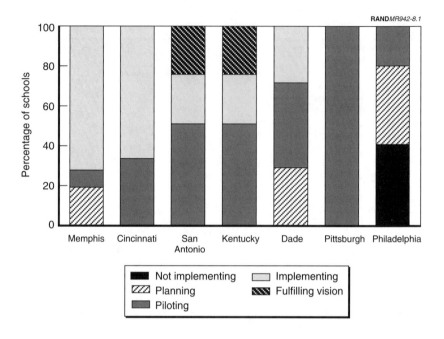

Figure 8.1—Jurisdiction Levels of Implementation: Five Elements

schools is important for understanding progress. In the remainder of this chapter, we will concentrate on the results for the different elements for schools among the year 2 schools.

Using these results, we can roughly sort jurisdictions into two general clusters: A greater percentage of schools in Dade, Philadelphia, and Pittsburgh were at low levels of implementation than in Memphis, San Antonio, Kentucky, and Cincinnati.

JURISDICTIONAL AND INSTITUTIONAL FACTORS CONSIDERED

In choosing this jurisdiction strategy, NAS went into uncharted waters; we do not know what a supportive environment is for design-based assistance. NAS has advocated specific structural changes, and each of the districts has attempted to put them in place. But the structural elements NAS advances are really working hypotheses of

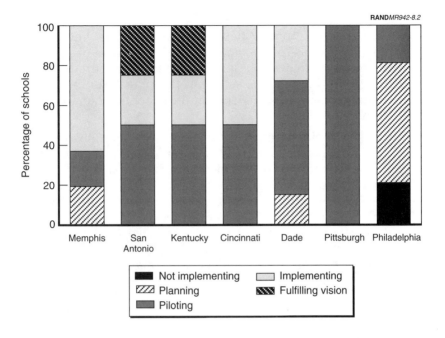

**Figure 8.2—Jurisdiction Levels of Implementation:
Eight Elements**

what a supportive environment for design-based assistance might be—they are not based on empirical evidence.

Thus, rather than imposing a definition, we used a more inductive approach to establish what is supportive. We asked the actors involved. We rely here on the point of view of school staff on which actions, policies, or conditions in the district supported their work and which did not.

Factors Considered

School staff were clear and forceful in their views on what district policies either supported or impeded their efforts. From their viewpoint, the following are the most important district and institutional factors that contributed to implementation:

- **Observed leadership support and central placement of the initiative.** The importance of the effort and therefore the level of priority it should be given was communicated by leadership actions (not just words). Central placement of the initiative is defined by staff as consistency of attention to the effort, actions taken to ensure that school staff understand its importance, lack of competing initiatives or setting a clear priority for this initiative, and perceived permanency of the superintendent or main advocate.

- **Lack of crisis situations.** Temporary crises that hit districts can often bump reform initiatives to a lower level of priority or draw resources, especially the time of leaders, away from the initiative. During interviews, staff often brought up the existence of specific types of crises in the district during the implementation period and the effects of the crises on their efforts. Note that this is a different level of crisis or tension than covered under the selection factors. Here, *crisis* meant budget crises, shake-ups in the Board of Education, political issues affecting the schools, court cases, labor-management disputes, etc. Note that there is

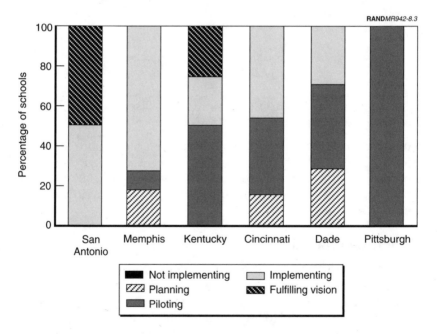

Figure 8.3—Jurisdiction Levels of Implementation for
Year 2 Schools: Five Elements

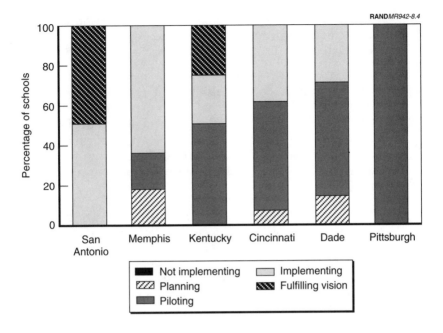

**Figure 8.4—Jurisdiction Levels of Implementation for
Year 2 Schools: Eight Elements**

a strong interrelationship between this lack of crisis and the perceived centrality of the effort.

- **Culture of cooperation and trust.** Some districts have strong
  positive relationships among management and labor; others
  have more dysfunctional histories. The history of trust was often
  cited as important in gaining acceptance and commitment to the
  initiative.

- **School level authority and/or autonomy.** This is defined as substantial control by the school over four areas: curriculum
  instruction and materials; personnel hiring, firing, transfer and
  positions; professional development; and budget. The level was
  determined both through interviews and review of budget documents.

- **Availability of resources for transformation.** Staff often noted a
  lack of resources as a barrier to implementation. Implementing
  a design requires adequate resources, as determined by the

stated needs of the design teams. The data on resource usage was collected from phone interviews and documents. We compared the amounts districts provided to schools for transformation.

- **Design compatible accountability and assessment systems.** This is defined by whether design teams or schools thought the design principles aligned with the assessment system of the district or state. We asked whether conflict had arisen between what the design demanded in terms of student learning and what the district or state demanded in terms of measuring student learning.

A quick comparison with the "supportive environment principles" in Table 2.2 shows some overlap between the factors cited above and those NAS advocates. School-level authority and autonomy, availability of resources, and compatible assessment and accountability systems are in common. However, more "political" factors of the role of leadership, the lack of crises, and the culture of trust did not enter into NAS's more structural view of a supportive environment. But these were cited as very important by teachers and principals.

Influence of Factors on Implementation Level

From the point of view of school staff, some districts were clearly more supportive of their schools' efforts to transform (see Figure 8.5). The districts are laid out across the horizontal axis based on the level of implementation rating determined by five elements in year 2 schools. As can be seen, there is a rough correspondence to the factors that school staff considered supportive and the ranking of the districts by implementation level. San Antonio and Memphis provided higher levels of support and had higher levels of implementation, while Dade, Philadelphia, and Pittsburgh were less supportive according to a school view and had lower levels of implementation. Kentucky had high levels of support but varied in implementation.[1]

---

[1]Datnow and Stringfield (1977) describe the Memphis strategy in great detail for those interested.

RAND*MR942-8.5*

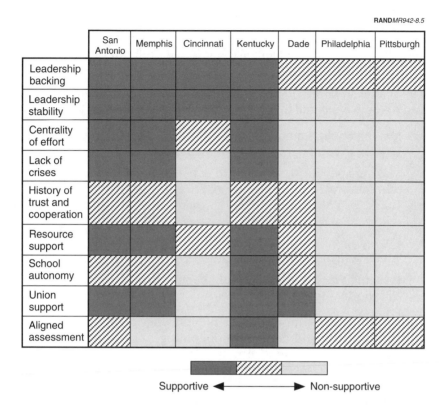

	San Antonio	Memphis	Cincinnati	Kentucky	Dade	Philadelphia	Pittsburgh
Leadership backing							
Leadership stability							
Centrality of effort							
Lack of crises							
History of trust and cooperation							
Resource support							
School autonomy							
Union support							
Aligned assessment							

Supportive ◄——————► Non-supportive

Figure 8.5—Schools' View of District-Level Support

Cincinnati falls somewhere in between. The following paragraphs provide the reader with real examples to illuminate the concerns of the school staff as they proceeded down the implementation path.

LEADERSHIP SUPPORT AND CENTRALITY OF EFFORT

Our school respondents in districts spoke in very different terms about the centrality of the NAS initiative and the observed leadership support, depending on their district. School staff in San Antonio, Kentucky, and Memphis reported firm leadership support in terms of the centrality of the NAS efforts to the reforms under way in the districts, the consistency of support by leaders, and the stability of the leaders themselves. Cincinnati was somewhat less so. From the point of view of teachers and principals at the end of the second year of the NAS initiative, the goals of the initiative, importance, and stability were far less clear in Dade, Pittsburgh, and Philadelphia than elsewhere.

The school superintendents in Kentucky, Cincinnati, Memphis, and San Antonio appeared to transmit clear goals and support for NAS by

- Making public statements and speeches, with backing from their Boards, to commit to the NAS initiative
- Making specific statements to schools, in personal visits and other forums, that whole-school reform was the way the district would go and that all schools would eventually adopt designs that were "research based"
- Changing school planning processes and policies to embedded whole-school design approaches
- Insisting that the schools would be judged on their results, usually within three years.

Perhaps more important from the point of view of the school, these communications and actions were coming from superintendents that, with the exception of one district in Kentucky, had been in office for at least several years and showed every sign of having strong political, business, and community support.[2] No one in those districts suggested to us that these superintendents were going away soon because of political pressures. Contrarily, many school staff noted that their superintendents' staying power was an important contributor to the reform progress made.

Taken together, these factors lent an air of immediacy and commitment to the NAS initiative in Cincinnati, Kentucky, Memphis, and San Antonio. Staff at the schools in these districts understood the effort to be central to the districts' efforts at improvement.

In contrast, school staff in Dade, Pittsburgh, and Philadelphia were comparatively much less sanguine about the NAS initiative in their

---

[2]At the time of the interviews, the positions of these superintendents appeared firm. At the time of this writing, Superintendent Brandt of Cincinnati had announced that he will be retiring because of health problems. This only underscores the tenuousness of any district reforms in light of the swift changes in leadership that typically occur.

districts and tended to report that the effort was not central to the districts' goals. Superintendents in these districts had used some of the same means of communicating the effort—but perhaps not with as much consistency, commitment, and associated policy changes as the above group.

As indicated above, the perceived permanency of the superintendent colored the message. Superintendents in Dade, Philadelphia and Pittsburgh appeared less stable in office to the school staff and more likely to "be leaving soon." The Superintendent of Pittsburgh announced her intention to retire in two years at approximately the same time she announced the NAS initiative, leaving teachers to question the district's commitment to NAS. The Superintendent of Philadelphia took on the union and others in his first three years in office in well-publicized battles. The press reported his imminent ouster, while the courts threatened to jail him for several actions. While he remains in office, many school staff understandably told us that they thought he would not last. The Superintendent of Dade County Schools left at the end of the 1996 school year, as did several key staff who had led the NAS effort.

In addition, each of these districts has recently rolled out major restructuring packages with new standards, assessments, and teacher and school evaluation mechanisms. These came at the same time as the NAS initiative. Thus, teachers reported they were hit with many competing priorities. While restructuring is happening in all the districts, the clarity of the communication of priorities in these three was reported to be lacking. More teachers reported not knowing where to place their priorities or how all the pieces fit together.

LACK OF CRISES

All districts periodically undergo strife and tension because of budget cuts, new political agendas, etc. This is a normal part of doing business, given the local structure of education governance. In our sample, Cincinnati, Dade, Philadelphia, and Pittsburgh underwent significant strife in the two years since the NAS initiative began. Each is facing a budget crisis of mounting proportions. In addition, Cincinnati and Philadelphia faced labor-management strife, while Pittsburgh faced an intensive redistricting debate. Dade has had to deal first and foremost with its growing student population, lack of building capacity, and the educational demands made by increasing numbers of students lacking strong English-language skills.

These crises or political issues tended to overwhelm the attention paid to NAS in those districts, making school staff skeptical of the centrality of NAS to their district's success or improvement or encouraging them to place it "on the back burner." In a specific example, two of the schools we studied in Pittsburgh in the first year would have been seriously affected had the redistricting plan gone through. Many teachers felt there was no reason to pursue reform until the redistricting issue had been decided. In the second year, they reported that the first three or four months of the year had been spent reducing budgets and reducing budgets again as the district sought to avoid a financial crisis. Under these conditions, school staff more often reported taking a "wait and see attitude" and assuming "this too will pass" than did staff in the other jurisdictions.[3]

CULTURE OF COOPERATION AND TRUST

Teachers in all districts talked of a "history of distrust" or a "path of broken promises" between the schools and the district. By this, they referred to a set of preexisting conditions in the district—not ones that were the result of the NAS initiative. While no district was free of this, a culture of distrust was almost palpable in several districts. Staff in Cincinnati, Philadelphia, and Pittsburgh mentioned such a culture most often. Teachers pointed to specific actions the districts had taken that fed this culture and made the teachers more likely to "take a wait and see attitude" toward design implementation.[4]

Some pointed to general tendencies indicating a lack of support for teachers' efforts. Specific indicators of commitment they cited were funding to reduce the number of students in their classrooms, to provide early interventions, and to increase the number of profes-

---

[3]This is completely consistent with the findings of Gitlin and Margonis (1995).

[4]Some might think that distrust of superiors is simply an attitude and has little relationship to behaviors in actual circumstances. Indeed, even in schools voicing distrust of the district, implementation was evident. But one line of research shows this distrust can have an impact on implementation (Brockner et al., 1997; Shea and Guzzo, 1987). Teachers in our sample said they had not participated fully because of this feeling of distrust.

sional development days offered. New state funding and rules in Texas, Tennessee, and Kentucky have promoted these efforts. Teachers in Dade, Philadelphia, and Pittsburgh, however, said they felt a lack of commitment by their superiors when they were asked to produce higher performances with a high number of children in classrooms and little in the way of additional professional development. These districts often have class sizes of 30 students or more. Allocated professional development days have remained constant or been reduced. Continuing budget crises in these districts force the continuation of this pattern. Cincinnati moved toward increased accountability without a significant increase in funding for professional development—teachers still provide volunteer time for professional development.

Others pointed to specific recent actions of perceived "about-faces" in district policy. For example, Pittsburgh announced to its schools that it would provide budget autonomy and eight days of professional development per teacher if they became NAS schools. Schools that signed up stated they did so at least in part to have access to much-needed professional development. The autonomy over the budget was never delivered (it is expected in the 1997–98 school year); by the second year, the extra staff-development days were rescinded because of a budget crisis. These changes in policy or lack of perceived follow-through on promises were seen as one more wedge in the social contract between the schools and the district.

SCHOOL-LEVEL AUTHORITY AND AUTONOMY

Schools need some minimal discretion or leeway from the many rules and regulations that govern schools if they are to be innovative and adopt designs. Our research from the Phase 2 demonstration schools indicated that certain types of autonomy were important.[5] These issues surfaced again in the scale-up phase as schools and design teams identified that schools need authority over the following to implement the designs well:

- curriculum, instruction, and schedules—to meet design specifications

---

[5]Bodilly et al. (1996), Chapter Six.

- the budget—to meet design requirements
- personnel—to create new positions, transfer non-supportive personnel to create a cohesive staff, and evaluate the staff against the new design practices
- professional development—to meet the identified needs of the design.

Districts varied in the degree to which they allowed schools the needed autonomy. Significant examples of barriers to implementation were reported in each of the above areas. The following paragraphs briefly describe a few examples in the areas of curriculum and instruction, reallocation of the budget, and personnel.

Authority Over Curriculum and Instruction

Examples of the lack of authority over curriculum and instructional practices largely fell into two categories: conflicts between the design and teacher-accreditation requirements, and conflicts between the design curriculum and district-mandated standards for curriculum content.

Some districts have adopted content standards that prescribe when a particular subject will be taught, or in effect prescribe a discipline-based approach. Several designs promote more interdisciplinary approaches or cover specific content at specified grade levels that do not match those of the district.

Multiyear instruction or interdisciplinary instruction sometimes conflicted with state teacher-accreditation requirements. For example, high school teachers in Dade were particularly reluctant to adopt interdisciplinary curricula because they were concerned about breaking state laws prescribing what each teacher could or could not teach.

In most cases, these types of issues could be worked out between the district and teams through a flexible approach to the design. This issue is connected to a scale-up strategy. Individual schools were not offered blanket exemptions. Instead, when districts committed to scale-up in many schools, these policies and their effects had to be reviewed carefully. Each design was reviewed for its effects, a process that was probably necessary in a scale-up but that also slowed implementation.

Authority Over the Budget

More-severe impediments to implementation involved the lack of school-level authority over the school budget and the inability to reallocate funds to the needs of the new design-based vision. Impediments to school control over the budget allocation can be as simple as state-level controls over funds used for textbook purchases, which discourage schools from purchasing the materials and texts the designs require in favor of those on state-approved lists. Or it can be as complicated as concerns over equitable allocation of funds among schools when school budgets are decentralized.

The districts involved stated they were moving toward "decentralization" of the budget to the school level—thus allowing schools autonomy over all their funding and potentially enabling schools to pay for the designs through internal budget reallocations. With the exception of Dade and the Kentucky schools, this decentralization of the budget had not been implemented. All districts had moved some funds in this direction—Title 1 funds or supplies and materials might have been given to the schools. But these funds could often only be applied to designated uses or were a small portion of the total school budget. As an example, while Philadelphia moved to school-based budgeting some time ago, the funds are still constrained to certain uses; schools have control, but only for use within certain categories.

Districts cited concerns about equity—in terms of the per-pupil expenditure varying by schools—as a major barrier to fully decentralizing budgets to schools. They put considerable effort into trying to come up with a "fair" way to decentralize the budget. NAS offered consultants to districts to help solve this issue. In the last interviews, representatives in Pittsburgh, Cincinnati, and Memphis reported that the NAS schools in the districts would pilot the move toward full school-based budgeting beginning in the 1997–98 school year.

Authority Over Personnel

To implement designs fully, schools often say they need stronger school-level control over positions within the schools, hiring, firing, and transfer. This is often prevented by state and district rules and regulations but can also be impeded by labor contracts.

State and District Impediments. Some districts or states mandate positions in schools by enrollment numbers. For example, some states or districts require a librarian, assistant principal position, or a counselor once school enrollment passes a specified level. Others have moved toward mandated reduced student-teacher ratios that prevent the movement of staff to other categories.

In every school that transforms, some teachers will not be supportive and will act to undermine the reform in the school. It then becomes important to have the ability to transfer the nonsupportive teachers out of the school. Some districts recognized this issue as potentially important and set up the means for dealing with it. In Memphis, for example, all teachers were required to sign a statement saying they supported the design. Those who would not sign the statement could be transferred. Those who signed and subsequently did not support its implementation could be transferred after due process. Indeed, Memphis principals reported the transfer of teachers under this policy. This system had been supported by the union, and as far as we know, no grievances were filed under it. In contrast, schools in Pittsburgh or Philadelphia with strong union regulations on seniority and transfer reported extreme difficulty in transferring nonsupportive teachers.

Labor Contract Impediments. This discussion has so far focused on state and district authority as the source of problems in gaining the needed minimal level of autonomy for schools to transform themselves. However, in some districts, school staff were just as frustrated with their union as they were with the central office. The issue schools raised most often was the inability to transfer or fire a person who did not support the design or to hire someone who did because of rules on seniority placement in the contract. In Pittsburgh, Cincinnati, and Philadelphia, school staff talked extensively about the barriers to implementation in the master contract or in specific union actions.

The school staff's view of the union and the impediments it created to reform had little to do with the statements of the union leaders in support of NAS. In fact, union leaders in most of the NAS partner districts had clearly stated their support. But language in the master contracts still imposed impediments.

AVAILABILITY OF RESOURCES FOR TRANSFORMATION

Implementing the designs requires resources or, at least, the reallocation of existing resources within the school. These resources are spent on the following types of costs: payments to the design teams for assistance, denoted as design costs; personnel slots within the school, such as a facilitator or a coordinator (personnel); training and planning time for teachers (teacher time); and materials and conference costs. The resources can come from different sources, depending on the districts.

The next few paragraphs cover the different levels of resource support districts provided to schools and some of the sources of those funds. Several districts (San Antonio and Memphis) provided significantly more resource support for the NAS efforts than did other districts; this influenced implementation.

Resource Availability

As part of our probing for the reasons behind the varying levels of implementation observed, we tracked the actual spending for each school and the variance from district to district in the different categories of costs listed above.[6]

Our analysis showed that average spending or resource allocation in all categories to implement a design in the 1996–97 school year was approximately $162,000; this includes some additional costs borne by the school or district and more significant internal reallocations of existing funds within a school. The variance among teams is significant, as indicated in a previous chapter.

The majority of the funds were spent on activities related to school personnel—paying the salaries of facilitators and coordinators (personnel—36 percent) or paying teachers for their time in professional development or planning (teacher time—40 percent), as shown in Figure 8.6. Fees to design teams themselves were a minor portion of the spending (16 percent).

---

[6]The collection and analysis of resource data were done by Brent Keltner and Robert Reichardt in a set of 45-minute to one-hour interviews with 58 schools in a sample drawn from Cincinnati, Dade, Memphis, Philadelphia, and San Antonio.

RAND*MR942-8.6*

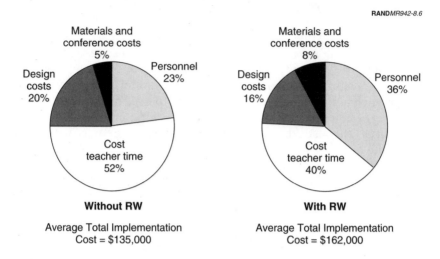

Figure 8.6—Average Implementation Spending on Designs

To examine district-level variation, we made a series of calculations to arrive at each district's mean resource contribution compared to the average contribution of other districts implementing the same design.[7] The findings, shown in Figure 8.7, suggest that, of the districts studied, San Antonio and Memphis have made the greatest per-school commitment of personnel and teachers' time. The average San Antonio school has committed 56 percent more personnel, 27 percent more planning time, and 14 percent more training days than the average of schools in all other districts implementing the same designs. The average Memphis school has committed 19 percent more planning time and 25 percent more training days, though somewhat fewer personnel than the average of schools in other districts.

---

[7]For each school in the sample, we normalized cost to that of an average size school. We then subtracted the level of personnel, planning hours, training days, cost of design services, and cost of materials and conferences from the average cost of all schools associated with the design. We then divided the variation from the average by the average itself to get a percentage variation. We then summed the percentage variation across all schools in a district and divided by the number of district schools in the sample. This provides an estimate for a particular district's variation from the cross-district mean cost of all design teams associated with the district.

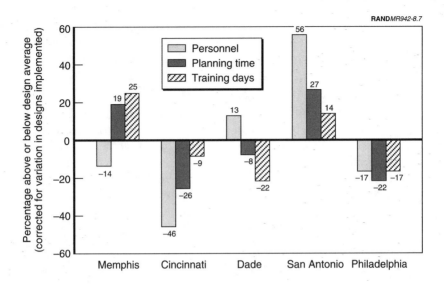

Figure 8.7—Relative District Resource Support for Implementation

Dade schools have made a reasonably high commitment of personnel resources, with the average Dade school committing 13 percent more personnel to implementation than other districts using the same designs. Dade schools, however, lag in committing teacher time. The average Dade school committed 8 percent less planning time and 22 percent less training time to design implementation than the average of other districts using the same designs.

Cincinnati and Philadelphia committed the lowest level of personnel and teachers' planning time. It is worth noting that the Philadelphia figures are largely driven by the low spending on AT designs. Seven of the eight Philadelphia schools in this sample are AT schools in their first year of implementation. All of these schools had lower levels of resource investment than their AT counterparts in Memphis.

Differences in the ability of schools in each district to reallocate teachers' time is a major driver of variation in the commitment of resources to training. Memphis and San Antonio schools appear to have considerably more freedom than their counterparts in Dade, Cincinnati, and Philadelphia to reallocate inservice days to design-team training. For example, inservice days in Dade are largely used at the discretion of the teachers; in Cincinnati and Philadelphia, the budget crises have reduced these days to a minimum. Most teacher-training time in Cincinnati is volunteered, again leaving usage up to teacher discretion.

Districts varied in their commitment of district funds to pay for the cost of design-related personnel, such as facilitators and coordinators. In Dade, the school district used Title 1 funds to help schools offset the costs of curriculum coordinators, technology coordinators, and reading tutors. In San Antonio, the school district used district Title 1 money (available in all schools in San Antonio) to pay for an "instructional guide" position at all elementary schools and state compensatory funds to pay for instructional guides at all secondary schools. Most NAS schools in San Antonio have used their instructional guides to assist in the implementation of the designs by acting as coordinators and facilitators. In short, district policy had already set up positions that schools could easily capture to implement the designs.

The ranking of districts by level of implementation corresponds closely with these findings on spending for implementation. San Antonio and Memphis provided the most consistent funding for implementation and achieved higher levels of implementation, while Cincinnati, Dade, and Philadelphia spent relatively less and achieved less implementation.

It should come as no surprise that schools in Memphis and San Antonio more often reported that the district supported the effort by providing the resources needed. In Cincinnati, Dade, and Philadelphia, school staff more often reported that the effort was underfunded and that the district was "nonsupportive" in terms of resources. In a preceding section of this chapter, we said that these same three districts faced significant budget crises during this period. Their actions can be interpreted as indicating that they were unable to support, rather than deliberately nonsupportive.

Finally, the differences in implementation that are due to different levels of district support were clearly responsible, from the point of view of school staff, for the differences in implementation among schools in Kentucky and in Pittsburgh. All these schools were part-nered with the NA design team. The state of Kentucky supported this effort with six full-time staff, and Kentucky districts supported it with

Goals 2000 funds. School staff stated that the effort was well-supported in terms of resources. In contrast, Pittsburgh did not provide the professional-development days promised, and its "district-level" facilitators—a key part of the implementation support—had other duties besides implementation of the NA design. Staff in Pittsburgh indicated that this observed underfunding sent a clear message that the effort was less important than other concerns and felt justified in reducing their emphasis on implementation.

Changing Sources of Funds

Going into this effort, NAS argued that districts should provide both school autonomy over budgets and significant investment funds for transformation. We have already indicated that most districts did not provide the autonomy NAS sought but are moving toward it. Some districts did provide substantial funds for investment in transformation, especially professional development and planning time.

Shifting from one source of funding to another during the middle of the effort proved problematic. Both Cincinnati and Memphis began with the district paying for significant portions of the design-based assistance. During the middle of the second year, as they prepared for a more decentralized budget, the central offices of these districts told the schools that the schools would have to bear the resource burden of design implementation in the third year. Schools reacted strongly to this change in policy. Some argued that they could not afford the costs of the design; indeed, in those districts, only schools with Title 1 funds had significant discretionary resources at that point to be able to "afford" the designs. Others argued that they would rather spend their resources on other items, especially more teachers per classroom, computers, or aides. But this shift in policy also caused further claims by school staff that the district was not to be trusted.

In contrast, San Antonio did not give schools the level of autonomy over the budget that NAS urged. The superintendent argued that the schools were not used to having discretion and would not know how to value the NAS designs. From the central office's point of view, it was better for the district to keep control of the resources but to make sure the effort was fully funded. This stance avoided the problems associated with "changing horses in midstream."

DESIGN COMPATIBLE ACCOUNTABILITY AND ASSESSMENT SYSTEMS

In our interviews, teachers often said that the tests the district administered and the manner in which the design teams were telling them to teach were in potential conflict. Many questioned whether the project-based, integrated, and problem-driven approaches they were being asked to use would result in test score increases on the particular set of tests being used by the district for accountability. Hidden in this concern are two issues:

- A conflict between what was being learned and what was being tested. Teachers in Cincinnati, Dade, and Memphis expressed concern that the district assessments were particularly inappropriate to the manner in which they were being urged to teach.

- The unproven nature of the instructional approaches advocated by the design teams. No matter the tests, teachers were concerned that the design teams and the literature offered no hard evidence that adoption of the proposed practices would improve student performance.

In several instances, teachers' concerns were motivated because their jobs, pay, or reputation were increasingly on the line if student performance did not increase. For example, the state of Tennessee created a system to track student improvement associated with the teacher, known as TVAS.[8] Within the next two years, teachers likely will be held accountable in their performance reviews for increasing the test scores of students—especially in reading and math. Similar situations existed or were about to be put in place in Cincinnati, Philadelphia, Pittsburgh, and San Antonio.

Teachers held accountable for reading and math scores are searching for ways to improve. The uncertainty associated with design-team practices made them fearful of adopting those practices, so some report falling back to "tried and true methods" of "skill and drill."

---

[8]The Tennessee Value-Added system of assessment tracks students over time by teacher to determine whether students under a particular teacher generally improved their performance to the desired grade level. In 1996-97, teachers in Memphis got the first results of this tracking—a computer printout showing whether they had enabled the "improvement" of students, as determined by the Tennessee system of testing.

Ironically, however, these are the methods that have produced the poor results on state tests.

School staff have offered ways to make their environment more friendly for implementation. They often suggested that they be "held harmless" on test scores for three to four years until they had been able to implement the designs fully. In addition, they and the design teams offered alternative assessments, better aligned with the designs, by which they could be judged. These included portfolios and student work products. None of the districts have agreed to hold schools harmless from test scores. The tests are often mandated by the state and not under the control of the district. However, several districts have said they would review other indicators of student performance provided by the schools, as well as the tests.

IMPLICATIONS

Analysis of districts and their effects on level of implementation showed that higher levels of implementation were associated with issues not identified by NAS as part of a supportive environment. In particular, political issues were often associated in teachers' and principals' minds with their efforts at implementation. Higher levels of implementation were associated with districts

- Whose leadership teachers perceived as being stable and strongly supportive of the effort and who communicated clearly how the NAS initiative fit in with other restructuring efforts under way

- That lacked political crises, such as a significant budget reduction, labor-management strife, or a redistricting debate

- That had a relatively stronger culture or history of cooperation and trust between the central office and the schools

- That provided some school-level autonomy, commensurate with that needed to promote the design

- That provided more resources for professional development and planning.

We also found that the assessment and accountability systems within the district were important. Teachers worried about their ability to adopt designs while improving test scores and meeting accountability levels. But the impact on implementation was less clear.

The slow and complicated nature of changing institutional arrangements described here is echoed in other implementation analyses and has been largely attributed to the complexity of changing interrelated organizations simultaneously.[9] In many instances, the move toward a more supportive environment was delayed by actions other than those of the districts, such as the rules and regulations of the states. The effort was delayed in several instances by overwhelming political issues, leadership turnover, elections, and crisis. Finally, at least some part of the pace of restructuring was due to the scale of the effort. Because all schools would potentially be affected, districts reviewed policies and practices extensively and deliberately. This took time.

The slowness of the effort should not take away from the progress made in all districts toward the reforms advocated. But the progress made so far should not be taken as leading toward certainty of results. The above examples point to the importance of the political nature of educational governance and the resulting difficulties districts have in steering a straight and consistent course toward reform.

---

[9]Pressman and Wildavsky (1973), Berman and McLaughlin (1975), and Hill and Bonan (1991).

Chapter Nine

CAVEATS AND CONCLUSIONS

From our observations, what one makes of the NAS initiative to date is open to judgment. About half the schools in our sample were making significant progress toward implementation at the end of the second year. Whether one considers this "good" or "bad" performance depends, of course, upon one's point of view and prior experience. If one is familiar with past reform efforts or with the difficulties of complex organizational change in the public sector, these results probably look quite positive. Seeing any movement at all in a two-year period, other than the adoption of a small program or adoption by some part of the school, can be considered strong progress. For those used to command-based organizations or to organizations free from the influence of local politics, these results might be frustrating, even bleak.

We think several issues should be taken into account before any judgments are made:

- This analysis was not based on a random sample. Selection biases exist for both districts and schools. Their exact nature is not known, but some were hinted at in the analysis of the selection process.

- The analysis performed here revealed high levels of interdependence between the independent variables. This reduces the ability to make strong statements of cause and effect but does provide the reader with a better understanding of the realities of reform. These realities should be taken into account by the reader.

- The implementation is only the first step in the process of transformation. The proof of the NAS approach is not in these data
  but will be in the next few years as it is determined whether this
  progress had permanent or fleeting influence on student performance.

- The proof of the approach will also be in how NAS, design teams,
  districts, and schools use their experiences to improve performance in the future and to develop even more effective
  approaches for reducing the proportion of schools that have not
  made significant progress in their implementation in the first
  two years.

Before proceeding, we would like to emphasize the future implications of the first and second bullets. NAS's approach and our
methodology, which is tailored to it, will affect our abilities to discern
and report clear cause-and-effect relationships in the future. We will
continue to add "pieces" of analysis to the picture to complete the
puzzle, but some issues will remain inscrutable.

THE COMPLEX PICTURE

We would summarize this analysis with a reminder of the larger picture that has been painted. We found many interdependent, inter-
connected factors to be important in supporting implementation in
the schools. These are summarized in Figure 9.1. They include
actions taken by schools, districts, states, unions, and design teams
in concert with each other and in conflict with each other. We found
that implementation levels varied significantly across the 40 schools
we studied.

Selection Process and School Climate Factors

We found that the initial selection process in most districts was hurried and did not always proceed as planned. All schools were
affected in some form or other by the timetable and the newness of
the effort to all parties. But some schools fared better than others in
this process. In particular, schools were likely to make more significant implementation progress within the two-year time frame we
studied if they

- were well informed about the designs

RAND*MR942-9.1*

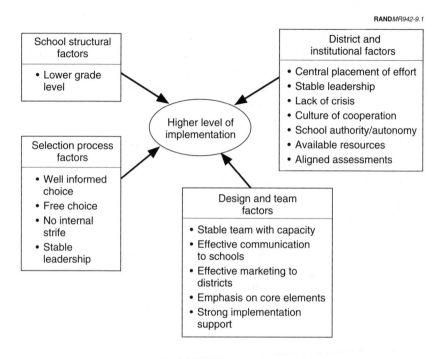

Figure 9.1—Factors That Support Implementation

- had a free choice among designs
- did not have significant internal strife prior to undertaking the design
- did not have leadership turnover during the two years studied.

The more of these factors that were not evident in a school and its selection process, the less likely implementation became.

The implication is that the selection process is important to implementation, at least in the time frame we studied. Design teams and districts should work to improve the process, and they appear already to be doing so. Just as importantly, the findings point to the fragility of the process and its easy corruption or displacement by other district and school priorities. The findings indicate that the care and maintenance of the initiative and clarity of direction must begin earlier rather than later.

Design and Team Factors

NAS intended to ensure that design teams developed into self-suffi-cient enterprises that could both assist high-quality implementation in schools and assist many schools simultaneously. Our observa-tions reveal that the designs varied in their abilities and capabilities to provide both quantity and quality over this period of time. Higher levels of implementation were associated with design teams that

- had a stable team with the capacity to field qualified personnel to serve schools
- effectively communicated their designs to schools and avoided school staff confusion
- effectively marketed to districts and gained the resource support required by the design
- emphasized the core elements of schooling common across the designs: curriculum, instruction, student assignment, assess-ments, and professional development
- supported implementation with whole-school training, facilita-tors, extensive training days, and common planning time.

School Structure and Site Factors

Our review confirmed a general finding of the literature on school reform: Implementation tends to be slower in the secondary grades than in the elementary grades. Stronger progress was made in alter-native or restructured secondary schools than in "typically" struc-tured secondary schools. Interviews with districts, design teams, and schools indicated that the design teams' efforts in developing the designs for the higher grade levels were not as strong as for the ele-mentary levels. This clearly implies that the work of the teams and NAS is not done. Our findings show that further development of the designs and specific interventions and strategies for the higher grades are needed.

Jurisdiction and Institutional Factors

Analysis of districts and their effects on level of implementation showed that teachers and principals thought both political and structural factors affected implementation. Higher levels of implementation were associated with jurisdictions

- Whose leadership teachers perceived as being stable, as strongly supportive of the effort, and who communicated clearly
- That lacked political crises
- That had a relatively stronger culture of trust between the central office and the schools
- That provided some school-level autonomy, commensurate with that needed to promote the design
- That provided more resources for professional development and planning.

In many instances, the move toward a more supportive environment was delayed by actions other than those of the districts, such as the rules and regulations of the states. The effort was delayed in several instances by overwhelming political issues, leadership turnover, elections, and crisis. Finally, at least some part of the pace of restructuring was due to the scale of the effort. Because all schools would potentially be affected, districts reviewed policies and practices extensively and deliberately.

OVERARCHING THEMES

Several overriding themes come from this analysis. These themes buttress, and are buttressed by, similar themes from other studies of implementing systemic change in public systems in general and in K–12 education in particular.

First, the effort at school reform is complex because of the multiple actors involved, no single one of which controls all the inputs needed to ensure implementation outcomes. Rather, the inputs needed for implementation are ensured through reiterative negotiations and extensive interactions over time. In short, the multiplicity of actors in the system targeted for change, their different levels of authority, and the complexity of joint action affect the pace of progress.[1]

---

[1] This finding is consistent with a long line of research in implementation encapsulated by Mazmanian and Sabatier (1983) but best described by Pressman and Wildavsky (1973).

Second, a corollary to this is that design teams by themselves do not accomplish implementation. Our analysis revealed a messy organic model of change, not a deterministic one. Importantly, in the model we observed, implementation progress was not the responsibility of a single change agent or a managerial function. Rather, what we uncovered is a model in which design teams can give schools and districts no guarantees of results because results depend at least in part on inputs that schools and districts control or contribute— resources, commitment, time, and effort. Schools will succeed at this effort, in part, because they and their districts choose to, not simply because of the services teams provide. Nevertheless, design teams can improve their capability in this regard.

Third, the effort appears to be difficult, and accomplishments are often fleeting, because of the political nature of the system in which it is embedded. Local community issues and district politics have a heavy influence that is unavoidable. Changes in leadership, budget crisis, etc., all have their effects and lead inevitably to "mutual adjustment" or "mutual adaptation" as actors seek to proceed given these types of constraints.[2]

The picture painted here reflects Wilson's (1989) view of schools as coping organizations buffeted by the political environment in which they function. Combining the above three points also reemphasizes Weick's (1982) view of schools as loosely coupled, fragmented organizations. In such organizations, change does not leap easily from one to the other, and the top cannot directly enforce the operators' behaviors because of the multiplicity of interactions and loose ties between different actors. The lower-level operators—teachers—are highly autonomous. Nevertheless, they are strongly influenced by past messages, the level of perceived support, and the permanency of the effort.

Fourth, the influence of leadership and the leader's role in a changing culture is implicit in these results. A stable leadership at both the school and district levels appeared to be important to teachers, as were clear signals about the priority to be placed on the effort. But it is the *observed* leadership by operators at the school level that proved crucial. They clearly looked for messages from leaders about the

---

[2]Berman and McLaughlin (1975) and Lindblom (1959).

importance of the effort and found messages in many different mechanisms, not just through the statements of leaders. To paraphrase Shein (1992), whose work this analysis echoes, the views of leaders were perceived through what they paid attention to, the ways they allocated resources, and who and what they rewarded. "Leaders communicate both explicitly and implicitly the assumptions they really hold."[3] Schools in at least several cases clearly perceived messages different from the ones the leaders claimed to have sent. Resource allocation is a particularly important message carrier.[4]

Fifth, two models of change are still to be found within the designs. One is keyed to quickly implementing task-level changes to core elements. Another is keyed to longer-term change, building school-level capacity to promote self-improvement. We have yet to evaluate all the implications of these two approaches fully. However, we recognize implications for the period of time over which they must be studied to understand their impact. The designs that have developed specific task and instructional practices for specific situations appear to be more readily implemented. Designs that rely more on the "professional" and "personal" development of the teachers to lead them to more effective task definition appear to be less readily implemented.

Sixth, resources for implementation were important in three ways:

- The ability of schools to gain access to "investment" resources signaled the leadership's priorities. Lack of investment funds was a clear signal of lack of leadership support.

- Autonomy over internal school resources was important for implementing design-specific changes. Without this autonomy, schools could not pay for design facilitators, coordinators, etc.

- The level and type of professional development were important and were controlled primarily by district policy. One implication of the above is that we can make no firm statements about the affordability of designs. In a real sense, the schools received the level of design-based assistance they were willing to pay for.

---

[3]Shein (1992), p 252.

[4]Weatherley and Lipsky (1977), Pressman and Wildavsky (1973), Mazmanian and Sabatier (1983), Korten (1980), and Montjoy and O'Toole (1979).

Finally, we have, in traditional fashion, attempted to separate the effect of the design from the effect of implementation. Distinguishing among these effects is no doubt important in the abstract. However, this research should fortify those who have found the two to be largely inseparable in practical observation. More and more, from our viewpoint, the design and its implementation strategy are becoming fused into a single unit. The design is its implementation in real schools.

Perhaps the most important lesson we have learned (and one we all learn over and over again) is that there still are no easy answers, no silver bullets. Elmore and McLaughlin (1988) had it right: K–12 reform is steady work. But this report also points to the tenuousness of that effort and ease with which the effort can dissipate. As McAdoo has indicated,

> small schools need big allies. . . . "Without more sustained, systemic support for the power of their ideas, they're always very fragile, and then people say they're not replicable."[5]

---

[5]McAdoo (1998), quoting Deborah Meier.

BACKGROUND HISTORY OF NEW AMERICAN SCHOOLS

This appendix describes the previous phases of New American Schools in more detail as background for the reader.

COMPETITION PHASE (PRE-1992)

In October 1991, NAS issued its RFP, which asked for "break-the-mold" designs that would integrate all elements of a school's life.[1] Respondents were encouraged to be creative, to ignore existing rules and regulations, and to create an innovative vision for new schools. NAS received over 600 proposals from all over the nation. After extensive reviews by panels of experts, 11 teams were awarded contracts.

At the time of the competition, teams were given guidance as to the rough amount of funding that would be available: up to $20 million per team for the five-year period. NAS planned to raise approximately $200 million for the effort and had already made some progress toward that goal.

DEVELOPMENT, PHASE 1 (1991)

During NAS Phase 1, teams receiving contracts were to develop their team and design concepts further to ready themselves for demonstration in real schools. The goal was to have well-developed designs and implementation strategies by the end of the development stage that would allow the teams to enter into the demonstration schools

---

[1] New American Schools Development Corporation (1991), p. 21.

of their choosing. In addition, the teams were required to submit plans that showed that they could take their designs to multiple schools in the scale-up stage. At the end of the development phase, NAS dropped two teams, largely because they did not present convincing evidence of the capability to scale up beyond their initial sites.[2]

Conceptually, the relationship of interest at this time was between NAS and the teams. It can be characterized as two sided. NAS provided money and guidance to teams, while teams provided NAS with plans, materials, and ideas on their designs. Nevertheless, by the end of this phase, all teams were still at work developing elements of the designs.[3] In large part, this reflected the ambitiousness of some of the designs, which covered such elements of schooling as social services in schools, new standards, and new assessment packages. But it also reflected the difficulty of developing designs that covered elementary, middle, and high schools, given the differences in culture and student needs in schools serving the different grade levels.

Teams were provided with funding depending on what they were trying to accomplish and the negotiated settlement between NAS and the team. At this point, funding became a major issue because NAS had not raised as much as it had hoped. Initial pledges had provided sufficient funds to support this phase, but plans for continuation depended on raising additional money. Planning for the demonstration phase was difficult because no one knew what level of funding would be available. Finally, a large grant from the Annenberg Foundation helped sustain the effort, and other private donors later provided more funds. In the end, contributions equaled about $120 million for the whole five-year period from development through two years of scale-up. This guaranteed that the teams could go on but with fewer resources than the hoped-for $200 million.

DEMONSTRATION, PHASE 2 (1993–1995)

In July 1993, NAS awarded nine teams two-year contracts to demonstrate their designs in two or more schools. Over these two years, the

---

[2]For an explanation of two of these original designs and why they did not go forward, see Mirel (1994), and Mickelson and Wadsworth (1996).

[3]We have characterized designs as having 12 elements in Bodilly et al. (1996).

nine design teams developed and refined their concepts in about 150 schools in 19 states. NAS goals for each team in the demonstration phase were straightforward: (1) finalize the designs, (2) demonstrate all elements of the designs in the sites, (3) refine the design team's implementation strategy to ensure the capability to scale-up, and (4) show some indication that the design led to increases in student performance.

The model of change for the demonstration phase is illustrated in Figure A.1 and contains three sets of actors—NAS, design teams and schools—with an intended outcome of improved student performance.

During the demonstration phase, the teams worked with partner schools to demonstrate the designs. The schools were often chosen quickly, through happenstance, because of personal connections with team members or on the basis of ability to transform quickly.

The school leaders were, however, willing partners—volunteers for the effort to demonstrate new ideas within two years. The teams often enticed the schools to work with them by providing money to the schools or by offering their assistance for free. The NAS awards given to a team for demonstration activities ranged from just under $2 million to over $5 million per year. These awards were to be used as the teams chose. The amount transferred to demonstration sites varied among teams from approximately 20 percent of their NAS funding to close to 60 percent.

RAND*MR942-A.1*

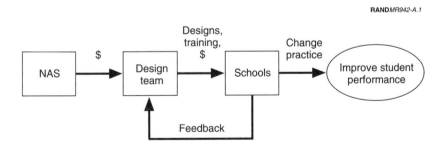

Figure A.1—Conceptual Framework of NAS Demonstration Phase

Analyses of implementation of the demonstration phase concluded[4] that design teams varied significantly in what they were able to demonstrate in schools in the two-year time period. Simply put, given the two-year time frame of NAS and the budget constraints, some teams were better suited than others to meet the goals of NAS. In addition, the districts that the teams worked in did not provide a supportive environment for the permanent transformation of individual schools that NAS sought. For a permanent change in the schools, the district would minimally have to provide incentives to adopt designs and the increased school-level autonomy needed to implement the designs. The most important legacy of the design teams at that point was not the designs alone, but the designs combined with the implementation "packages," which we called design-based assistance. It was only with both the design and the assistance that schools were able to transform. Finally, all designs needed further work and were incomplete. Most importantly, a great deal of work remained to be done by teams on the designs of secondary schools, and the elements of social services integration and governance.

At the end of the demonstration phase, NAS dropped two teams, Community Learning Centers and Los Angeles Learning Centers, from participating in the scale-up phase. Los Angeles Learning Centers was encouraged to continue developing its design.

---

[4]Bodilly et al. (1996).

DESCRIPTIONS AND DESIGNS

The following are descriptions of each of the designs, relying primarily on the elements defined in Bodilly et al. (1996). The elements are used as appropriate. In all cases, we cover the core elements of standards, curriculum, instruction, assessment, student groupings, and professional development. These are then followed by organization and staffing, governance, community involvement, social services, and technology. The design teams originally described their designs in 50-page documents and specified the details of the designs in subsequent submissions to NAS. The latest attempts at documenting the designs were through the benchmarking process. While these brief paragraphs do not do justice to the designs, we hope they capture some of the essential traits of each.

AUTHENTIC TEACHING, LEARNING, AND ASSESSMENT FOR ALL SCHOOLS (AT)

The design assumes that high-performing schools are not possible in the current bureaucratic structure. The intent of the design is to move schools away from "the bureaucratic reality to the authentic vision" of education. The design aims to change the culture of the schools to promote high institutional and individual performance. Four beliefs about the purpose of schools drive the design. Schools are to

- help students acquire valuable habits of heart, mind, and work
- help students develop deep understandings
- use only activities that are developmentally appropriate
- create a community of learners.

Design Team Leader: Linda Gerstle

Pathway/Governance: The concept of an autonomous pathway is the key to the design because it frees a contiguous group of schools from constrictive governance structures. Equivalent to a feeder pattern that is coterminous with a community, the pathway must be self-governing, requiring formal changes in the governance structure of the district.

Standards: Using the new governance structure, each pathway will rethink what a high school graduate should be able to do. From this reconception, it will develop its own standards of performance for each grade level through the committees. Standards will be based on performance and outcomes and will be explicitly stated and public so that the community can join in judging the efficacy of the schools.

Curriculum: The curriculum moves away from emphasizing the accumulation of a broad set of facts to emphasizing in-depth understanding of the world. For example, in high school, many electives and lecture formats would be changed to fewer courses with more in-depth experiences. The curriculum is organized by themes called "essential questions." Answers to the questions are explored in an interdisciplinary fashion. Teachers use the ATLAS curriculum planner to develop more meaningful courses. The ATLAS Communities Team and other study groups align the curriculum across the K–12 feeder pattern to ensure that the agreed upon standards are met.

Instruction: Instruction is highly personalized, with attention to individual capabilities and maturation rates. This is reinforced by a personalized school structure with fewer students per teacher.

Assessments: The pathway creates exemplary exhibitions for graduates and benchmarks for key years. Assessments are authentic in that they must be based on demonstration and performance. There is strong support for portfolios to be used over time to demonstrate student development and maturation. Publicly reviewed exhibitions are used to assess students' performance before graduation.

Student Groupings: The design will promote multiage grouping as appropriate and will avoid pull-out programs. Cooperative learning will be emphasized. Tracking will be avoided.

Professional Development: Teachers become a stronger force in the school by creating their own professional development plans, being responsible for research and development of new curricula and instructional strategies, and being members of the governance teams. Personalization will be promoted through opportunities for collaboration and support for training including networking among teachers and the establishment of teacher study groups.

Organization: Schools within a pathway will be managed by School Planning and Management Teams (SPMT). In each school this team will be supported by school-level teams, a Community Health Team, a Teacher Team, a Parent Program, and a Student Program in each school. All will work to support the SPMT. Members will represent different important voices in the community. Decisions will be made by consensus with free, no fault discussion guided by a process developed by the School Development Program. The pathway will be managed by the ACT and use the same consensus processes.

Staffing: Schools commit to fewer students per teacher, such that high school teachers would have no more than 80 students.

Community Involvement: Ancillary services, such as mentoring, speaker programs, and volunteers, are provided by community members. Community members are also active participants on the school governing teams and the schools develop programs to encourage parental involvement. The school will work with the community to survey and map the community assets and develop a plan to use them more effectively to support learning.

Integrated Social Services: Schools closely coordinate with social-service providers through the Community Health Team. Members from this team sit on the SPMT to ensure community health issues are heard.

Technology: Computers will be used in the classrooms to aid in personalized instruction. They will also enable communication within schools and across the pathway, cementing the relationships needed to build a community of learners.

AUDREY COHEN COLLEGE SYSTEM OF EDUCATION, ALSO KNOWN AS PURPOSE-CENTERED EDUCATION (AC)

The design is based on a holistic approach to education centered in developmentally appropriate curriculum. The curriculum and instruction are organized around a single, developmentally appropriate purpose for each semester, cumulating to 26 purposes in a K–12 system. For example, kindergarten is dedicated to the exploration of "We build a family-school partnership" and "We care for living things." Embedded in each purpose are content areas, such as English and math, and essential skills, such as critical thinking and researching. Each purpose culminates in a constructive action taken on by the class to serve the community. These fundamental changes in the curriculum and instruction become the organizing principles for all other school activities. The total effect is intended to make the school and its programs more coherent and focused.

Design Team Leader: Janith Jordan

Standards: The school will meet existing state standards, but every school will also have the standards developed by the Audrey Cohen College, which align and support the purpose-driven curriculum.

Curriculum: During each semester, students focus all learning and activities on a single preassigned purpose. Traditional subject areas and important skills are absorbed by action-oriented dimensions: acting with purpose, weighing values and ethics, understanding self and others, understanding systems, and making use of skills. The semester culminates in a constructive action that has been determined by the students and is directed toward improving the world outside the classroom. Secondary students serve internships in the community.

Instruction: The classroom is opened up to the community, and teachers become leads for their students' activities. Speakers and volunteers for different purpose-related activities visit classrooms and provide students with real-world applications. Students visit their communities for their purposes in a greatly increased number of field trips. Learning becomes more hands-on as students learn through interactions with the world around them.

Assessments: Although schools continue to use existing standardized tests as required by the district and state, the design team has also developed a framework of demonstrable abilities and skills for each grade. Teacher-developed assessments are embedded in the curriculum and match the specific purpose of each semester. Students use the Purpose Note Book provided by the team for their own self-assessments. Student work and products are the focus of assessments, not tests.

Student Grouping: Students will be grouped in ways appropriate to the purpose and constructive action of each semester. This should result in more group-learning modes, cooperative learning, and mixing of ages. The design is intended to promote learning by all students.

Professional Development: Teachers, principals, and administrators organize their jobs around the purposes and begin to build bridges between the school and the outside world. Grade-level teams work together to exchange ideas and develop appropriate an curriculum at a regularly scheduled time. Teachers from across Audrey Cohen schools work together and exchange ideas in a developing network.

Staffing: The design requires the creation of a staff resource position to gather materials and make contacts in the community, to peer-coach teachers in the classroom, and to serve as a liaison with the design team. Teachers are responsible for planning the curriculum as a collaborative team. Administrators remove barriers to making the school more coherent and build bridges to the community to support the purposes.

Governance: This design does not require significant governance changes other than those given to magnet or theme schools. However, significant governance changes can result from the incorporation of purposes as the focus of schooling.

Community Involvement: The purposes help the school and its officials identify key community resources to involve in the educational enterprise. The constructive actions help bring the community into the school and the school into the community—making schools, parents, and children active partners in improving the community. The constructive actions benefit the community and affect it in positive ways to improve community harmony and function.

Integrated Social Services: The design specifies that coordination with community and health-service agencies is accomplished at the school level, as appropriate for that community. The curriculum makes student awareness of health issues and contact with health-related agencies an organic part of the curriculum.

Technology: Networked classroom computer centers, studios for television and photography, and other technology provide students access to information and the means for developing work products. Technology is also applied to the management of record-keeping tasks.

THE CO-NECT SCHOOL DESIGN (CN)

The design calls for a dramatically different learning environment for students, teachers, and the community. The design was originally targeted at middle school children in urban settings; however, it has grown to other grades and settings. In addition to understanding key subject areas, graduates demonstrate the acquisition of specific critical skills, identified as sense-maker; designer; problem-solver; decisionmaker; communicator; team worker; product-oriented worker; and responsible, knowledgeable citizen.

Design Team Leaders: Bruce Goldberg, Bolt Berenek, and Newman Associates

Standards: The school's design team begins its efforts by examining standards and developing a school-based standard with input from the community and with the aid of CN associates. Standards will exceed current expectations for students from urban areas. The benchmarking process the design uses helps schools set goals for meeting standards, reviewing progress, and adjusting curriculum and instruction appropriately.

Curriculum: The design features a school developed, project-based curriculum that is product oriented and supplemented by seminars and workshops in skills and other areas. The curriculum will be multidisciplinary and will use cluster-wide investigations.

Instruction: Students follow a personal growth plan developed by teachers, parents, and the student together. They work together in appropriate groupings, depending on the task. Instruction becomes more technology-based with students accessing worldwide resources through computer technology.

Assessments: Separate performance assessment frameworks provide the basis for a continuing process of setting goals and measuring progress for individual students and groups and for the school as a whole. The design relies on a mix of assessments and portfolios to judge students. The school develops exemplar products and rubrics to guide student assessments.

Student Grouping: The school is ideally organized into multiage, multiyear clusters of students with the goal of low student–teacher ratios, but schools can choose more appropriate groupings. Tracking is abolished.

Professional Development: Professional development is viewed as an ongoing process. CN teachers promote their own professional development and have access to a network of professional development services and materials. Professional development will be project oriented, with teachers learning by doing. Teachers can be judged by the demonstrated work of their students. "Critical friends" visits among CN schools build a critical and collegial network of practitioners.

Organization: A council with broad membership—teachers, parents, business and community representatives, and administrators—manages the school. In addition, a school design team provides local input concerning the implementation, performance assessment, and accountability of the CN approach at that particular school. Finally, the community-support board fosters access to the local community in support of the council and the design team.

Staffing: The school will have fewer students per teacher, and teachers will remain with students for two to three years. Staff will be organized in multidisciplinary teams.

Governance: The design does not specify particular governance relationships between the school and the district.

Community Involvement: A community-support board will help the school interact with the community at large. Mentoring and volunteering are encouraged and community input sought for standard setting.

Integrated Social Services: Counseling and referral will be provided. Teacher teams will work closely with students to provide support.

Technology: A technological infrastructure supports student access to knowledge and local, national, and global resources; the creation of student products; and the management of personal growth plans, résumés, and portfolios.

EXPEDITIONARY LEARNING (EL)

The design engages students and revitalizes teachers through a teacher-guided, project-based approach that focuses every aspect of teaching and learning toward enabling all students to meet rigorous academic standards and character goals. Curriculum, instruction, assessment, school culture, and school structures are modified to produce higher-quality student work. The school's culture and structures are transformed to support powerful teaching and high achievement for every student. Teachers and school leadership participate in a rich sequence of professional-development activities that enable them to implement the design effectively. Annual review of school progress, based on Expeditionary Learning benchmarks that assess the level and quality of implementation and are grounded in evidence of learning outcomes, drives continuous improvement.

Design Team Leaders: Meg Campbell, Greg Farrell

Curriculum and Standards: The curriculum is based on learning expeditions—long-term, in-depth investigations of themes or topics that engage students in the classroom and in the wider world through authentic projects, fieldwork, and service. Learning expeditions are designed and planned with clear learning goals that are aligned with and meet or exceed district and state standards. These expeditions are the primary vehicle for students to learn the skills and habits of mind they need to master and are, therefore, an important part of an effective strategy to prepare students for mandated tests.

Instruction: Instruction emphasizes hands-on experiences and fieldwork with student learning through greater interaction with the community and real life experiences. Teachers are guides to learning; formalized lectures and didactic approaches are reduced. Block scheduling becomes the norm as students work for protracted periods on projects.

Assessment: The design calls for authentic assessment, including performance-based exhibitions, student portfolios, and student self-assessment. The assessments reinforce learning by encouraging drafting and redrafting of student work products until they meet high standards. Student work products are shared with the community to ensure they meet community standards and to encourage support.

Student Grouping: The design eliminates student tracking and mainstreams special education students. Using a multiyear approach, students stay with the same teacher for two to three years to create a more stable teacher-student relationship and to keep the teacher better engaged through the change in grade level every year. Within classrooms, students commonly work in small groups to build social skills and to learn the value of everyone's contribution.

Professional Development: Staff development is considered the key activity in building a curriculum. The design approach emphasizes treating teachers as professionals by empowering them to create expeditions. Staff development is built around activities that increase the confidence and enthusiasm of teachers to become learners themselves and that provide teachers with resources and ideas to build curricula. Teachers work in teams to build networks of practitioners. They are allotted significant time for working together during the school day. In groups, teachers engage in peer review of each others' curricula and teaching practices.

Organization/Governance: The design does not require any formal changes in the governance or organization structure but does advocate a decentralized structure adopting a web-management approach, in which administrators provide resources and coordination to assist the specific needs of teachers and the school. School-based management is encouraged.

Staffing: The design requires no changes to staffing. Professional apprenticeships and master-teacher approaches are encouraged.

Community Involvement: Community involvement is not the emphasis of the design but is promoted indirectly through the off-site nature of the expeditions, the requirement for community service as part of the curriculum, and the need for student internships. Mentoring and volunteering are promoted.

Integrated Social Services: The design advocates school-based social supports for students and outreach programs but does not require specific interventions.

Technology: Technology will be incorporated as appropriate. No specific technology is required.

MODERN RED SCHOOLHOUSE (MR)

Guiding the MR design are several principles and assumptions, including the following:

- six national goals for education
- all students can learn
- a common culture that is represented by a core curriculum and generic competencies
- principals and teachers with the freedom to organize instruction
- schools accountable through meaningful assessments
- use of advanced technology to achieve results
- choice in attending an MR.

Design Team Leader: Sally Kilgore

Standards: The design develops its own unique set of world-class standards for all students that reflect high expectations associated with Hirsch's Cultural Literacy curriculum for students in the elementary grades and with workplace competencies and Advanced Placement tests for students in the intermediate and upper grades.

Curriculum: The design advocates a curriculum founded on Core Knowledge. Core Knowledge will account for about 50 percent of the curricula, allowing leeway for a school's own curricular emphasis. The elementary students make use of Hirsch's Cultural Literacy curriculum, which is sequenced in a year-by-year fashion. In this design, teachers reorganize their curricula into themes used across grades and integrated across subjects and make use of computer technology. Hudson Units are a means of "capturing" curricular units and connecting them into a holistic system of standards, assessments, content, resources, and pedagogy. Students' performance on a "collection" of Hudson units is expected to add up to mastery of MR world-class standards. Teachers develop Hudson units with guidance by the design team.

Instruction: The design advocates the more flexible use of time so that all students can meet standards. Instruction would be self-paced. Students preferably would be in heterogeneous, multiaged clusters with the same teacher for several years, although this is not required. Instruction would emphasize methods to promote student problem solving and thinking. Acknowledging that all students are capable of learning, albeit at different paces, the MR design calls for students to engage in self-paced learning and to organize their learning efforts in accordance with an Individual Education Compact (IAC) negotiated by the student, parents, and teacher.

Assessments: Student performance is measured by various MR-unique assessments, including tests, watershed assessments, and embedded assessments. Schools are expected to adopt the MR standards and assessment package.

Student Grouping: This design promotes appropriate multiage, multiyear groupings with few pullouts. New instructional strategies will promote individualized instruction and multiple regroupings during project work.

Professional Development: The designers have conceived a two-part strategy. The first part calls for MR to train teachers to implement core features of the design. The second part is the establishment of a self-sustained professional-development program designed at the school level.

Organization. In the first year of implementation, the school staff organizes into five teams. These teams then develop plans for their issue areas and subsequently work together to manage the school. Multiple teams within the school ensure more teacher participation and the participation of those outside the school.

Staffing: The designers advocate an MR teaching force comprising adults from a wide variety of backgrounds. Implementing school autonomy over teacher selection and hiring and curricular change makes this possible.

Governance: The design requires extensive school-level autonomy in the areas of curriculum and instruction, standards and assessment, budgeting, hiring and staffing, and outsourcing of services. The team attempts to negotiate this up front with the district.

Community Involvement: This is not a heavily emphasized element in the design; involvement is encouraged especially through volunteers and business partnerships.

Integrated Social Services: Based on assessment of a school's community by one of the school teams, implementing schools are expected to engage social agencies operating locally to assist "at-risk" pre-K though grade 12 students. This is a district responsibility, although an expert consultant will facilitate site efforts. The school's primary emphasis will be on education. It is expected that community services agencies will provide services. The team offers booklets and materials to support parents of preschool children.

Technology: The design includes a schoolwide computer network and installation of multiuse microcomputers in classrooms. Teachers will use classroom computers to track students' progress through Hudson Units and IECs. Students use the computers for instructional and information-access purposes.

NATIONAL ALLIANCE FOR RESTRUCTURING EDUCATION, ALSO KNOWN AS AMERICA'S CHOICE (NA)

Instead of promoting change school by school, NA provides a framework for all levels of the education system (state and local education agencies, as well as schools) to support restructuring of schools. The vision is based on the belief that systemic change requires a combination of top-down and bottom-up strategies. NA intends to combine member sites and outside experts into a networked umbrella of unifying tasks and goals in five core areas.

Design Team Leader: Judy Codding

Standards and Assessments: Originally, all NA sites were members of the New Standards Project (NSP), a collaboration of the National Center on Education and the Economy, NA, and the Learning Research and Development Center at the University of Pittsburgh. The effort went beyond NA, with a total of 20 states signed on to the project. NSP is both developing new standards and incorporating existing high standards in an outcomes-based system of assessments.

NA sites agree to keep indicators of progress, known as "vital signs," to measure whether sites are moving toward the goals of systemic change. Two kinds of measurement are being developed: changes in terms of student performance and indicators of changes in student experiences.

Districts and schools that are part of NA are encouraged to adopt the Certificate of Initial Mastery and to use performances and portfolios with well-understood rubrics to assess students.

Learning Environments: The design sponsors a number of initiatives aimed at enhancing the curriculum, professional development strategies, and instructional resources to increase learning in school. The task is an amalgamation of what used to be three separate components of the design: curriculum and instruction, school-to-work focus, and technology as an important part of instruction. The task is intertwined with the NSP in that learning outcomes provide the starting point from which teachers develop units of study.

Fundamental to the task is the emphasis on improving the learning environment through professional development opportunities that involve interactions among lead teachers and principals in schools and experts outside the school through a variety of networking devices. Professional development is keyed to developing leaders.

All students are detracked, and flexible groupings are encouraged. The curriculum includes technical literacy, applied learning tied to school-to-work standards, and the development of interdisciplinary units of study. These are supported by materials and training opportunities from NA.

Community Services and Support: NA sites are tasked with developing better ways to integrate health and human services with the schools to serve children's emotional, physical, and academic growth. The task is outcomes based, keyed to agreed-upon descriptions of what communities and schools want for children, such as students coming to school ready to learn.

High Performance Management: NA sites adapt for education the principles and techniques developed by American business known as "high-performance management." They work to restructure the organization and management of schools, school districts, state departments of education, and the policy systems in which they work by adapting the effective business practices of the most successful American firms. Such practices include putting the resources and decisionmaking authority in the hands of those who work most closely with students, providing appropriate support, and holding all accountable. Principals and teachers are trained in these principles and practices so that they may better support the integration and implementation of the design tasks.

Parent and Public Engagement: NA assists partners in finding better ways to foster sustained public support for the systemic changes in policy and practice that are prerequisites for achieving world-class performance at all levels of our education system. This design task also involves helping parents focus on the academic achievement of their children and helping them provide the conditions necessary for success.

Evolving Design: The specific work subsumed under each of these design tasks continues to evolve—to deepen—over time with the needs of its partners. For example, in one year, a major focus was on the further development of a school-to-work model and on the design of the high school of the future. Another year, NA focused on building a fuller understanding of standards, assessments, and rubrics and their connection with curriculum and instruction via standards-driven units of study. Currently, NA is deepening its work through standards-based networks by providing practical training and support to teachers in using core assignments as building blocks in a fully standards-based curriculum. It also provides school leaders with an understanding of how the structure and organization of the school must change to create an environment in which the standards-based practices can flourish.

ROOTS AND WINGS (RW)

The design is intended for elementary schools with Title 1 funds. The "Roots" component of the design intends to prevent failure. It emphasizes working with children and their families to ensure that children develop the basic skills and habits they need to do well in succeeding years. The "Wings" component emphasizes a highly motivating curriculum with instructional strategies that encourage children to grow to their full potential and aspire to higher levels of learning. The means of accomplishing both components lies in manipulating existing resources in the school, especially Title 1 funds, to provide better instruction and support.

Design Team Leaders: Robert Slavin, Nancy Madden

Standards: The design goal is to improve the performance of all students, by raising the average performance and reducing the number of low performers.

Curriculum: The structure of the curriculum will change to encompass three components. First, the schools will use an improved *Suc-*

cess for All component for reading and writing skills. The design team is also providing a math component modeled after the reading component and incorporating new standards from the National Council of Teachers of Mathematics. Finally, much of the rest of the day will be devoted to an interdisciplinary, hands-on component called World Lab, which integrates science, social studies, math, language arts, and key skills.

Instruction: Problem-solving modes and group-learning process will require different teacher instructional styles, moving away from being a lecturer to being a guide. Learning will become more activity based. Tutoring is provided as needed. Block scheduling is required for the three curriculum components. Individual Education Plans are encouraged for all students, with parents involved in the process.

Assessments: Assessments will be increasingly performance based with hands-on demonstrations and portfolios. The strategy is to position Roots and Wings schools to perform increasingly better on assessments evolving as part of a national move toward improved outcomes, rather than to develop a set of assessment tools unique to Roots and Wings.

Student Grouping: Pullout programs will be eliminated as special teachers, volunteers, and others work in the classroom or after school with students who need additional help. During some parts of the day, homogeneous groupings of students will be used for developing specific skills, say reading. Rather than permanent assignment to a group, each student will be assessed and reassigned to new groups, as appropriate, every eight weeks. The idea is to provide individual attention to those who need it so that they can move from one group to another as they progress. Groupings for math would be different from groupings for reading. During World Lab and other parts of the school day, children will be in heterogeneous groups working in problem-solving modes.

Professional Development: The role of the RW facilitator after implementation is to provide release time to teachers, assemble materials, observe teachers' instruction, suggest improvements, and model the design elements.

Organization: The design encourages a participatory school improvement team with the principal acting as chief executive officer. The design facilitator and family-support coordinators would participate on this team.

Staffing: The design includes two new staff positions in the school: a family-support coordinator and a Roots and Wings facilitator to ensure the design is established and maintained.

Governance: The design encourages, but does not require, site-based management and relies on the ability of the school to control internal allocations of discretionary federal and state funds.

Community Involvement: The family support coordinator is responsible for developing volunteers in the schools, structuring the before-school and after-school programs to address individual needs, making home visits to families with children in need, and in general ensuring that children come to school ready to learn.

Integrated Social Services: The focus of ties to the family and community services is on infants, toddlers, and school-age children. Social services will be coordinated through a site-based team run by a family support coordinator at each school (possibly through the reallocation of Title 1 funds) and facilitated by a district move toward more-integrated services.

Technology: The instruction requires additional computer and other resources to provide students with access to hands-on instructional software and educational resources. However, computers are not a central piece of the design.

BIBLIOGRAPHY

Adelman, Nancy, and Beverly Pringle, "Education Reform and the Uses of Time," *Phi Delta Kappan*, September 1995, pp. 27–29.

Berman, Paul, and Milbrey McLaughlin, *Federal Programs Supporting Educational Change, the Findings in Review*, Santa Monica, Calif.: RAND, R-1589/4-HEW, 1995.

Bidwell, Charles, Kenneth Frank, and Pamela Quiroz, "Teacher Types, Workplace Controls, and the Organization of Schools," *Sociology of Education*, Vol. 70, No. 4, October 1997, pp. 285–307.

Bodilly, Susan, Susanna Purnell, Kimberly Ramsey, and Christina Smith, *Designing New American Schools: Baseline Observations on Nine Design Teams*, Santa Monica, Calif.: RAND, MR-598-NASDC, 1995.

Bodilly, Susan, Susanna Purnell, Kimberly Ramsey, and S. J. Keith, *Lessons from New American Schools Development Corporation's Demonstration Phase*, Santa Monica, Calif.: RAND, MR-729-NASDC, 1996.

Brockner, Joel, et al., "When Trust Matters: The Moderating Effect of Outcome Favorability," *Administrative Science Quarterly*, September 1997, pp. 558–583.

Cuban, Larry, "A Fundamental Puzzle of School Reform," *Phi Delta Kappan*, January 1988, pp. 341–344.

Cuban, Larry, "Reforming Again, Again, and Again," *Educational Researcher*, Vol. 19, No. 1, January 1990, pp. 3–13.

Daft, Richard, "Bureaucratic Versus Non-Bureaucratic Structure and the Process of Innovation and Change, *Research in the Sociology of Organizations*, Vol. 1, 1995, pp. 129–166.

Datnow, Amanda, and Sam Stringfield, "The Memphis Restructuring Initiative: Development and First Year Evaluation from a Large Scale Reform Effort," *School Effectiveness and School Improvement*, Vol. 8, No. 1, March 1997.

Elmore, Richard, and Milbrey McLaughlin, *Steady Work: Policy, Practice, and the Reform of American Education*, Santa Monica, Calif.: RAND, R-3574-NIE/RC, 1988.

French, Wendell, and Cecil Bell, Organizational Development: Behavioral science Interventions for Organizational Improvement, 3rd ed., Englewood, N.J.: Prentice-Hall, 1984.

"From Risk to Renewal: An *Education Week* Special Report," *Education Week*, February 10, 1993.

Firestone, W., S. Fuhrman, and M. Kirst, *The Progress of Reform: An Appraisal of State Education Initiatives*, New Brunswick, N.J.: Rutgers University, Center for Policy Research in Education, 1989.

Fullan, Michael, *The New Meaning of Educational Change*, New York: Teachers College Press, 1991.

Gitlin, Andrew, and Frank Margonis, "The Political Aspect of Reform: Teacher Resistance as Good Sense," *American Journal of Education*, No. 103, August 1995, pp. 377–405.

Herman, Rebecca, and Sam Stringfield, *Ten Promising Programs for Educating Disadvantaged Students: Evidence of Impact*, Center for the Social Organization of Schools, Johns Hopkins University, Presented at the American Association Research Association Meeting, April 19, 1995.

Hill, Paul, and Josephine Bonan, *Decentralization and Accountability in Public Education*, Santa Monica, Calif.: RAND, R-4066-MCF/IET, 1991.

Huberman, A. Michael, and Matthew Miles, "Rethinking the Quest for School Improvement: Some Findings from the DESSI Study," *Teachers College Record*, Vol. 86, No. 1, Fall 1984, pp. 34–54.

Korten, Daniel, "Community Organization and Rural Development: A Learning Process Approach," *Public Administration Review*, September/October 1980, pp. 480–511.

Levin, Henry, "Learning from Accelerated Schools," unpublished paper, Accelerated School Project, Stanford University, December 1993.

Lindblom, Charles, "The Science of 'Muddling Through,'" *Public Administration Review*, 1959.

Lippman, Laura, Shelley Burns, and Edith McArthur, *Urban Schools: The Challenge of Location and Poverty*, Washington, D.C.: National Center for Education Statistics, U.S. Department of Education, 1996.

Mazmanian, Daniel A., and Paul A. Sabatier, *Implementation and Public Policy*, with a new postscript, Lanham, Md.: University Press of America, 1989

McAdoo, Maisie, "Buying School Reform: The Annenberg Grant," *Phi Delta Kappan*, January 1998, pp. 364–369.

McDonald, Joseph, "Humanizing the Shopping Mall High School," *Education Week*, April 5, 1995, p. 46.

McLaughlin, Milbrey, "The RAND Change Agent Study Revisited: Macro Perspectives and Micro Realities," *Educational Researcher*, Vol. 19, No. 9, December 1990.

Meier, Deborah, "Can the Odds Be Changed?" *Phi Delta Kappan*, January 1998, pp. 358–362.

Mickelson, Roslyn Arlin, and Angela L. Wadsworth, "NASDC's Odyssey in Dallas (NC): Women, Class, and School Reform," *Educational Policy*, Vol. 10, No. 3, September 1996, pp. 315–341.

Mirel, Jeffery, "School Reform Unplugged: The Bensenville New American School Project, 1991–1993," *American Educational Research Journal*, Vol. 31, No. 3, Fall 1994, pp. 481–518.

Montjoy, Robert, and Laurence O'Toole, "Toward a Theory of Policy Implementation: An Organizational Perspective," *Public Administration Review*, September/October 1979, pp. 465–476.

New American Schools Development Corporation, "Designs for a New Generation of American Schools," Request for Proposals, Arlington, Va., 1991.

New American Schools Development Corporation, *Bringing Success to Scale: Sharing the Vision of New American Schools*, Arlington, Va., September 1995.

Newman, Fred, *Authentic Achievement, Restructuring Schools for Intellectual Quality*, San Francisco, Calif.: Jossey-Bass, Inc., 1996.

Policy Studies Associates, Inc., *School Reform for Youth at Risk: An Analysis of Six Change Models*, Vol. I: *Summary Analysis*, U.S. Department of Education, 1994.

Powell, Arthur, Eleanor Farrar, and David Cohen, *The Shopping Mall High School: Winners and Losers in the Educational Marketplace*, Boston: Houghton Mifflin Co., 1985.

Pressman, Jeffrey L., and Aaron Wildavsky, *Implementation: How Great Expectations in Washington are Dashed in Oakland; or, Why It's Amazing That Federal Programs Work at All This Being a Saga of the Economic Development Administration as Told by Two Sympathetic Observers Who Seek to Build Morals on a Foundation of Ruined Hopes*, Berkeley: University of California Press, 1973.

Prestine, Nona, and Chuck Bowen, "Benchmarks of Change: Assessing Essential School Restructuring Efforts," *Educational Evaluation and Policy Analysis*, Vol. 15, No. 3, Fall 1993.

Schwarz, Paul, "Needed: School-Set Standards," *Education Week*, November 23, 1994, p. 44.

Sebring, Penny Bender, et al., *Charting Reform: Chicago Teachers Take Stock*, Chicago, Ill.: Consortium on Chicago School Research, 1995.

Shea, Gregory P., and Richard A. Guzzo, "Group Effectiveness: What Really Matters?" *Sloan Management Review*, Vol. 28, No. 3, Spring 1987, pp. 25–31.

Shein, Edgar, *Organizational Culture and Leadership*, 2nd ed., San Francisco, Calif.: Jossey Bass Publishers, 1992.

Shields, Patrick M., and Michael S. Knapp, "The Promise and Limits of School-Based Reform: A National Snapshot," *Phi Delta Kappan*, December 1997, pp. 288–294.

Sizer, Theodore, *Horace's School, Redesigning the American High School*, New York: Houghton Mifflin Co., 1992.

Smith, Marshall, and Jennifer O'Day, "Systemic School Reform," *Politics of Education Association Yearbook*, 1990, pp. 233–267.

Smrekar, Claire, "The Missing Link in School-Linked Services," *Educational Evaluation and Policy Analysis*, Vol. 16, No. 4, Winter 1994.

Stringfield, Sam, and Amanda Datnow, "Scaling up School Restructuring and Improvement Designs," *Education and Urban Society*, Vol. 30, No. 3, May 1998, pp. 269–276.

Stringfield, Sam, Steven Ross, and Lana Smith, *Bold Plans for Restructuring*, Mahwah, N.J.: Lawrence Erlbaum Associates, 1996.

Stringfield, Sam, et al., "Introduction to the Memphis Restructuring Initiative," *School Effectiveness and School Improvement*, Vol. 8, No. 2, 1997, pp. 3–35.

Summers, Anita, and Amy Johnson, *A Review of the Evidence on the Effects of School-Related Management Plans*, Conference on Improving the Performance of America's Schools: Economic Choices, National Research Council, National Academy of Science, Washington, D.C., October 12–13, 1994,

Turnbull, Brenda, "Using Governance and Support Systems to Advance School Improvement," *The Elementary School Journal*, Vol. 85, No. 3, 1985, pp. 337–351.

Tyack, David, "Restructuring in Historical Perspective: Tinkering Toward Utopia," *Teachers College Record*, Vol. 92, No. 2, Winter 1990, pp. 169–191.

Usdan, Michael, "Goals 2000: Opportunities and Caveats," *Education Week*, November 23, 1994, p. 44.

U.S. Department of Education, *America 2000: An Education Strategy*, Washington, D.C., 1991 (revised).

Weatherley, Richard, and Michael Lipsky, "Street Level Bureaucrats and Institutional Innovation: Implementing Special-Education Reform," *Harvard Educational Review*, Vol. 47, No. 2, May 1977, pp. 171–197.

Weick, Karl, "Administering Education in Loosely Coupled Schools," *Phi Delta Kappan*, June 1982, p. 673.

Wilson, James, Bureaucracy: *What Government Agencies Do and Why They Do It*, New York: Basic Books, Inc., 1989.

Wohlstetter, Priscilla, "Getting School-Based Management Right, What Works and What Doesn't," *Phi Delta Kappan*, September 1995, pp. 22–24.